From Gaslight to Satellite

From Gaslight to Satellite

Frederick C. Holt

The Pentland Press Limited
Edinburgh • Cambridge • Durham

First published in 1994 by
The Pentland Press Ltd.
1 Hutton Close
South Church
Bishop Auckland
Durham

ISBN 1 85821 142 5

Typeset by CBS, Felixstowe, Suffolk
Printed and bound by Antony Rowe Ltd., Chippenham

Introduction

This is an attempt to give you a story of my lifetime and I propose to call it *From Gaslight to Satellite.* I have been encouraged to do this by my son, Peter, who as a young lad when he was a schoolboy used to jump into my bed on a Saturday morning and, of course, the idea was to tell him a story and, having spent nearly eight decades in my lifetime, I have probably got quite a lot of interesting stories to tell. The attempt is to try to illustrate to you the thoughts of my life so that, by the time we get to the end of the book, you will have had something interesting to read. So *From Gaslight to Satellite* is an illustration of my life span.

I was born in the era of gas light and here we are in the satellite era of my life, so this is the story dedicated to my son, Peter. My thanks are also due to my wife, Joyce, who has given me great encouragement and assistance in preparing this book.

CHAPTER ONE

I was born on 10 March 1916 in what could be called the eastern part of London, in Eastham in a street called Caleden Road and I suppose it would be typical of what one sees on Coronation Street. My father was serving in the Royal West Kent Regt. and was fighting in France in the Battle of the Somme. My earliest recollection is that at two years of age at the end of the First World War we moved to a two-bedroom flat above a greengrocer's shop in North Street in Barking, in what was then called Bonny Downs. This was all we could afford at this time as my father had just returned from the War and, like all soldiers, he had very little return after four years of fighting and we had to struggle on with what we had. I was the first of a family of four over the next five years. I suppose it is very difficult to remember things that happened at two years of age but I can always remember one amusing little incident. As you know in those days we had outside toilets – there were no facilities like you have today – and we had a little chamber-pot under the bed. I can remember as a little child calling my mother in and saying, 'Mum, there is something swimming around in the pot', and there was a little mouse, still alive, swimming around gaily trying to get out.

As I say, this is the first instance I can remember of this wonderful world we live in. From that stage I can remember various things – my mother not getting on with her neighbours and I can also recall going to the local pub with my father where we used to sit outside with a glass of lemonade and an arrowroot biscuit while he enjoyed this time inside with his friends. Women, of course, were not allowed in public houses then; these were purely the confines of the male population. My next move was to a home in King Edward Road. As a matter of fact the house we lived in is still in existence, once again typical of Coronation Street type of houses, very closely knit together and I have great memories of this place – I can remember moving at four years of age and our things were transported by donkey and cart. With what furniture we had we moved into what could be called our own home with a back garden and I can vividly remember sitting on the old donkey and cart while we drove the few miles we had to go to our new home. This provided us with two bedrooms, a so-called parlour, and kitchen. These were the days, as I say, of gaslight and this was the only type of light we had, and our cooking was done on a coal-fired stove in the dining-room. Our only means of communication was a cat's whisker crystal radio and I can still recall listening to some radio news which was '2 L O calling'. Everybody had to be completely silent while the earphones had to be fitted into our ears as we listened to the news available in those days.

All our washing was done by means of a fired copper. Once again, our toilets were outside in the garden.

The gramophone had to be wound up on a spring. So these were the days I was introduced to as a young lad. On Friday nights the massive, big tin bath was brought in front of the fire for the children. I was coming onto five years of age. Over this period of time my mother had four children. I had a younger brother, Len, and two sisters, Vera and Eva. Sadly to recall they have all since died and (I will be coming to this later) only two days ago my last sister, Vera, died in Essex in England.

However, we were all a very happy family. My father worked then at the Beckton Gasworks; I think he worked for the fabulous sum of about £3 per week – out of which he had to pay rent, and look after a wife and four children. There was no question of cars then. You might see one or two cars running about but everything was delivered by horse and cart; milk was delivered by the can, our coal was delivered by the sack, and our bread was brought by a van which was propelled by horse and cart. So it was a very slow life; a day would seem like eternity, a week would be forever, not like today where everything is very fast moving.

These were the days when washday was on a Monday when the copper was lit, and then on Tuesdays the steam puddings were put into the copper to be boiled. As I said, we had no electricity, but we had a life we enjoyed as I suppose we knew nothing different. Holidays were virtually out of the question. We were lucky if we went away for one or two days a year and that probably involved going out picking blackberries down at Averley. We enjoyed ourselves with our friends, and our mates at school, who were all from the local area. Schooldays were nothing spectacular; I was not what you would call a brilliant child – I suppose average to medium. I got through my schooldays under, I suppose, a little bit of resistance but I can still recall the various teachers, even their names, and getting the odd caning for being naughty or being late. I always had a respectable fear for the local copper, the policeman, the bobby who used to come around and was not afraid to box our ears and send us home if we did something wrong. I always had a great respect for our teachers and masters because I suppose the fear of the cane and of other punishments we might get. Today these sorts of things would be frowned upon, but when I look over my life and what I went through I don't think the fear of the cane and the local bobby, who was always around, did us any harm at all. At least we were able to walk about and do things safely then. So this is briefly how our schooldays were spent and our lives were spent.

Our shopping was done at the local greengrocer and corner shop. We bought everything in bits and pieces. You can imagine cheese being cut off to the amounts we required; if we wanted some pickles we took our own jars down to the shop. Everything was weighed out separately from a sort of bulk bin and this is how we did our shopping in those days. There were no such things as supermarkets or big stores or anything like that. We had a local cinema. I can still remember the first sound film of Al Jolson and going to see *Sonny Boy*, also the silent films of Charlie Chaplin and the Wurlitzer organ coming up from the floor in front of the stage, on which someone used to play the background music for the various films that were showing. It used to cost us something like a penny and I know that on a Saturday afternoon when we went to our other cinema, called The Electric, which was in High Street in Barking, we used to pay twopence to go and see Hoot Gibson or Ken Maynard, the old cowboy films, Richard Dix and Tom Mix and his wonderful horse. We would get a packet of sweets when we went in for our twopence, and we used to have a wonderful time. We used to sit there spellbound watching these actors chasing the Indians across the prairies of the mighty USA. As I said before, these were, in my opinion, great days. I was made to go to church every Sunday and I became very, very involved in the Church as I grew up in my early teenage years before I went to work. I was in the, choir being a fairly good singer. Being an Anglican we had a wonderful church in Barking – St Paul's – it had a marvellous atmosphere. I remember the minister was a Reverend Bridgestock to whom I became very, very closely attached. I was confirmed and went to church three times a day and thoroughly enjoyed this. I used to go to church gatherings in an evening where we used to make such things as leather bags, straw baskets and such like to raise funds for the church. I was so involved then I could never understand if I heard people using bad language or doing things which were outside of the religious life. The minister came along to my parents and asked if I could be taken into the Church but, of course, as I was the eldest and coming on to being the next breadwinner in the household and assisting with the finances of the home, my parents were reluctant to let me do this. Whether this was good or bad I don't know, but I would have willingly gone in those days. I am jumping the gun a little but this is just to give you a little idea of just how religion affected me at the time and how much I enjoyed it.

We stayed at King Edward Road until I was around eleven years of age and it was during that time that the marvellous innovation of electricity came along. In those days gaslight was used with a meter in which you put a penny for your supply. The machine only took pennies. Every so often the mantle had to be changed for the lighting, but then came along electricity and suddenly we found, that instead of the street being lit by gaslight every evening at twilight, now we had wonderful electric light replacing this, and we had electric light in the home. This was a great innovation; there were certain things we could use with electricity rather than relying on the normal manpower. In those days we were allowed to use as much electricity in our homes as we liked for 1/6 per week so if an electric light was put on it was never turned off. We got to the stage where we couldn't go to bed or sleep unless the light was left on. 1/6 per week was quite good for what it provided. We could then start looking at a new type of electric radio and various other things around the home. So that was my life span at King Edward Road until I was about eleven or twelve years of age.

New council houses (we call them state houses here in New Zealand) were being built and, because of the size of my family and the fact that everybody was growing up, we were able to apply then for a new home that was being built in Barking on the fringes of the area, at that time in a road called Ripple Road. This is densely populated now but I can remember when we moved into this house there were fields at the back and fields in the front, and the area going down towards Dagenham and Rainham was all fields. We were virtually the last house on the fringes of Barking. Needless to say that today you can travel for miles and miles further on and there are still houses and businesses and factories and what have you. This was a brand new home. It was what we called a two and a half bedroom – two double bedrooms and a single room and it had the usual lounge parlour and all the mod cons. The toilet was still outside but only just – being attached to the outside of the house. The bathroom was of a similar nature. We had to have a copper to heat our water – instant water from Ascots didn't come along until later years. The Ascot was an instant type of water-heater heated by gas.

My father acquired an allotment and grew all his own vegetables. These plots were available for about ten shillings a year and together with our small garden he was able to supply all the vegetables for home use so our standard of living became much better. All our family grew up from this house and my mother and father stayed there until they passed away. On a recent visit to England I passed the house and it is still as good as when built. I carried on my schooling at my old school. As I only had two years to finish my education and I had been there since I was five years old there seemed no point in changing. It was a two-mile walk and we had no means of transport.

CHAPTER TWO

When I left school the economy was very depressed; large unemployment and low wages and fourteen was the standard age for leaving school so things did not look too good at all. My father took me to London to a labour exchange where I was able to get employment as a page-boy in a commercial hotel in Aldersgate Road in Cheapside. This was part of a chain of hotels run by R.E. Jones. The hotel catered for business people from Europe. It was a very busy hotel and a page-boy's job in those days consisted of taking luggage to rooms, opening doors, working lifts and doing general messages for the customers. My uniform was tight fitting, dark blue with brass buttons and a bell-top hat. For all this I was paid ten shillings a week, but was able to secure tips for service that we gave the clients, like collecting luggage, calling taxis, opening doors, etc., and was very surprised at the amounts I received over the week. This averaged at around two pounds ten shillings which made up a very good wage. This was almost as much as my father earned as a shift worker at Beckton Gasworks so our standard of living jumped dramatically by the eldest son's income. On top of this I was fed at the hotel. Unfortunately this only lasted for about a year as being quite a chubby lad and still growing the uniform I was wearing was getting too small for me so the management took the lesser of two evils and decided it would be less expensive to sack me and employ a smaller edition, so yours truly was out of work again.

Once again my father took me to the labour exchange in London. I'll never understand why I was taken to London to get work but he must have known that the opportunities were better there. However, I was able to get employment at a French restaurant in Berkley Square in the

West End of London. This was as an apprentice. The name of the restaurant was Gunters. They had outlets in Bond Street, Sloane Square and Landsdowne Square. In the Victorian era, and at the time I worked there, anybody of class always dined at Gunters for light meals, coffee etc., and you can still pick up a Victorian romantic novel and see Gunters mentioned. I often tell people that I worked in Berkley Square when the nightingale sang and this is true. This would be the year 1933 also in the Victorian era where the nineteenth century still prevailed. Bruton Mews, a building, remained the same with its small park in the centre of the Square and, although I didn't recognise them as nightingales then, you could always hear the birds singing. I had an occasion to go back to London recently and have a look at the old place where I once worked and you would not recognise it. The restaurant had gone and in place of the lovely old buildings were tall modern ones. The only thing that remained was the small park in the centre of the Square – nothing like the romantic Berkley Square that I knew. This is where I learned the art of French pastry cooking – brioche, parmiers, croissants, petit fours, gateaux, etc. This was something I enjoyed and became good at. As I have mentioned before, Gunters was a very high-class restaurant and only the well off could afford to eat there. To give you some idea, Gunters supplied all the food for Buckingham Palace garden parties and wherever the Royal Family went, such as Ascot and Goodwood races. Gunters supplied the food for society weddings and balls, so it was the 'in thing' to have Gunters supply all the catering no matter what the cost. I used to attend some of these functions earning the princely sum of 5/- an evening and my weekly salary was 7/6, and although I could get a monthly season ticket on the train for about 8/6 a month it was necessary to try and do this journey on a cycle. This meant riding 50 miles each day (25 miles each way). This took me through Eastham, Stratford, East India Dock Road and Aldgate. In 1933 all these roads were cobblestone so you can imagine what sort of journey this was. I used to do this five days a week and sometimes have a dip in the Serpentine. Thinking back I must have been very fit and this must have prepared me for the trials that were to come. Of course one had no choice – if you wanted work you had to go no matter where. I stayed at Gunters until I was eighteen years of age (1934).

The manager called me into his office one morning. My apprenticeship had finished and if I stayed he would have had to pay me a full wage so he took the least line of resistance and replaced me with another apprentice, but because of my ability he gave me a recommendation to a professional employment agency to see if they could find me an occupation in the same trade. So off I went to this agency in Leicester Square. Once again work was very scarce; the only vacancy they had was for a fully qualified French pastry cook at a place called the London Tavern but they said perhaps I was too young for the job. I said couldn't I be the best judge of this and have the opportunity for an interview. They saw no harm in this and I must admit I was very young for this particular appointment and if I was successful I would have to pay the agency one week's wages.

London Tavern was situated in Fenchurch Street and it serviced the area which contained all the Stock Exchange and banking establishments which were the hub of the city of London. The London Tavern could cater for 1,500 customers and it had about seven different restaurants in the same building. Each room was named, such as King's Room, Queen's Room, Buffet, Grill, etc., and each room was built in marble on masonry and had a wonderful atmosphere. On arrival I introduced myself to the manager who in turn took me to the Head Chef for the interview. After a lengthy discussion they took me to the kitchen and told me I had the full use of the facilities and I was to prepare half a dozen items for their inspection. I then set about preparing items that would be used in association with a full dinner menu. This included baked jam rolls, steamed pudding, bakewell tarts, decorative jellies, etc. After about three hours I called the Head Chef back to inspect my work and they set about tasting the various items and looking at the presentation, and, being satisfied with what I had done, gave me the job on the spot.

This turned out to be quite an achievement as I was to have at least four men working under me, all of whom were old enough to be my father. There were no problems here – I was accepted because of my ability to do the job which turned out to be very interesting. I was responsible for the sweet menu which would consist of four hot and four cold items. I was paid the sum of two pounds ten shillings with some overtime doing carving at Lord Mayor's luncheons and at Temple Bar and also attending Masonic events and Regimental dinners.

On some of these occasions I had to lead in the haggis and flaming Christmas pudding. These were usually piped in with the piper leading followed by me in my check trousers and tall white hat, and ten waiters. On placing my tray at the head of the table, a toast was either given to the haggis or Christmas pudding and I was given a large whisky, together with the guests, to toast. I can assure you that neat whisky and eighteen years of age were not compatible. However, as a ritual I had to partake and the important thing was that I was being paid for the effort. It was about this time, getting to around the age of twenty that I had very little time for enjoyment, working hard five and sometimes six days a week, and with no catering act, hard work and no play made life seem very dull.

CHAPTER THREE

It was at this time, watching other people getting some enjoyment that I decided to give up catering and went to find work in Barking. I asked my father if he could get me a job at Beckton Gasworks, and being a carbonising foreman I hoped that he could pull a few strings. However, all I could get was casual work on a daily basis. This meant going to the place of work at shift work times, i.e., 10 in the evening, 2 p.m. or 6 a.m. It must be understood that unemployment was very high and sometimes fifteen or twenty people would turn up hoping to get a day's work and it turned out you would on average get three days work a week. The work was very hard and I could not imagine conditions of work such as these being allowed today. I did finally get myself into a full-time situation.

It was at this time I joined the Territorials. This increased my income as I was paid for attending training and it gave me a fortnight away each year on training on full pay. North Thames Gas Board had outlets all over London and employed about 30,000 people, so the Rangers, which was a sister regiment of the King's Royal Rifle Corps, was completely made up of employees of the Gas Board. By this time Hitler was getting very boastful and, with threats of dominating Europe being made, our training became more active and as we approached 1939 war became inevitable. It was on the twenty-ninth of August 1939 that all Territorials were told to report to Headquarters. Hitler had marched into several countries in Europe and England's involvement seemed imminent. My brother, who was also in the same unit, decided that we had better let our parents know that we had been called up. They were in Worthing on holiday at that time so we sent them a telegram reading as follows: 'If you want to see your sons before they go to war you had better come home now.' They were home the next day and then off we went to Chenies Street which was our Headquarters just off Tottenham Court Road in London – little did we know we were going to be there for the next three months, so our parents did see a lot of us before we went to war.

From there we were transferred to Richmond where we had plenty of open space for training for action. From there we went to Brigg, Lincolnshire where we were allowed mechanical transport such as a 30-cwt. truck, scout cars, Bren gun carriers, etc. Training was intensified and we were now in the depths of winter. I obtained promotion up to a full Corporal and Acting Sergeant and was an instructor in P.T., light 2" mortar, Bren guns and also driving instructor, so life became very interesting.

From Brigg we were transferred to Sawston in Cambridgeshire awaiting action abroad. This was about the time of the Battle of Britain. We could watch London burning from where we were stationed. I did have occasion to have leave at this time and arrived home at Barking. By this time London was being bombed every night. Everybody had air-raid shelters in their gardens and those who lived in the City used the tube stations as their shelters. At 6 p.m., when the sirens sounded, my mother and father said they were going to the shelter and this brave soldier said he would go to bed. Within half an hour mobile naval guns were firing outside the house. Artillery guns were banging away in the park and bombs were dropping all around us. It was not long before I was at the air-raid shelter telling all to move over, 'I'm coming in.' When one looked in the daylight at the damage that was being done and the killing that took place it made one wonder how London survived three years of bombing. The London folk were truly a great bunch to survive this.

While we were stationed at Sawston our weekends were our own to do as we wished. We could travel into town but had to be back in Camp by 11 p.m. each night. On one particular weekend my section (which consisted of eight men) said they would like to go to London to visit their wives and sweethearts. No permission could be given, but I allowed them to go on the understanding that I knew nothing about this venture and that they would take the consequences if they were found out; so they all left at midday on the Saturday but had to return before Reveille at 6 a.m. the next Monday morning.

Our camp was situated in a forest just outside Sawston and all the tents were camouflaged with creosote. Each tent contained one NCO and his Section. On this particular Saturday I went for a trip to Cambridge, arriving back before 11 p.m. and went to my tent and retired for the night. At about 1 a.m. I felt very hot, so much so that I awoke to find my tent engulfed in flames with me inside! I quickly escaped from the tent and called for assistance. None was forthcoming as everyone in the surrounding tents was fast asleep so I started dropping the tent myself. By this time, because of the commotion, help did arrive and the fire was put out. All our personal belongings, plus uniforms and rifles were in the tent and of course these were all destroyed. I relate this incident so that you can image the surprise on the faces of my Section when they sneaked back into Camp on the Monday morning and couldn't find their tent. Because of all this I had to report their absence over the weekend and they were all charged - poor guys! The only conclusion the authorities could come to with regard to the fire was that someone passing had thrown a cigarette alongside the tent. I was questioned very closely but, being a nonsmoker and not carrying any matches, I was considered blameless.

Hitler at this time was taking all before him. Norway had fallen and our troops in France were unable to stem the advances that the Germans were making. We were being prepared to go to France but because of the speed of the German advance and the French lines being broken, the race to get the British Expeditionary Force home was on. We all know of Dunkirk but that is a story on its own. By this time we had moved to Northants ready to be despatched abroad. It was about this time I became interested in the piano. As a lad of eight years I had had piano lessons, which I did not enjoy, so after four years of trying my mother gave up. As I got into my teens I started to take an interest again and developed a style of my own and as the War advanced I did a lot of playing in the local pubs of the area.

One amusing incident occurred when I was having a drink one night (this happened to have been market-day when all the farmers came to town to sell or buy their wares, cattle, etc.) and the pub was full. Each time a group had a round of drinks one was sent over for the pianist. Everybody sang songs and had a great time so much so that at closing time a cap was sent around with the remark, 'Come on – he only gets a bob a day' and I finished up with a farmer's cap full of pennies and silver. I played the piano for pleasure and not for gain but can assure you the money came in very handy.

From then on it was all go – the battalion was taken to Liverpool where we embarked on the *Strathallan* which was a cruise liner converted to a troop-ship carrying about 3,000 troops. The whole 60th Division was leaving and this involved six troop-ships plus escort ships. We had no idea where we were going but assumed that it was somewhere in the Middle East because of the size of the movement. This trip took about five weeks – going through the South Atlantic; stopping at Sierra Leone for refuelling and food, and then on to Durban where we spent Christmas 1941. We slept in hammocks, all the way. We managed to dodge all enemy ships. We were told the *Graf Spee* was chasing us but, apart from this incident and some very rough seas, we arrived at Durban intact. Entertainment on board was all done military fashion – tug of war, boxing etc. I was down to fight a regular soldier in an inter-battalion boxing match, so I set about training for this fight as a light heavyweight and my trainer was a local professional. On the day of the weigh-in I was a pound overweight so had to stand down and another person took my place. I went as a spectator and saw my stand-in get a first-class hiding. I think I was very pleased to be a spectator that day. My poor stand-in was in bandages for some time; the chap he fought was a real slugger with cauliflower ears and a broken nose.

Durban was a welcome change, very warm and the locals treated us very well. We had to be careful what we said whilst there as there were quite a lot of loyal Hitler supporters about. However, we had no problems and set sail for our destination which looked more like Egypt every day. We sailed through the Red Sea and Suez Canal on to Alexandria. We set up camp about twenty miles from Cairo where we got straight into desert training. We were convinced by this time we would be fighting in the desert. Life in the desert was one big army depot – thousands of troops from all countries. All we could see was sand and more sand. Every time we ate or drank anything it was contaminated with sand. Training was very hard; we had to learn to survive without water and we would be taken on a daily route march in the intense heat with empty water-bottles. The strange thing was, although it was very hot during the day it was the reverse at night – we needed several blankets to keep us warm. The NAAFI provided us with entertainment, open air films, canteens, etc. I did get a couple days leave in Cairo.

Whilst I was in the desert I received an assignment to teach a group of Indian NCOs in the use of the Indian light machine-gun. This was a replica of our Bren gun. This was a highlight of my stay in the desert. I would be collected by an Indian chauffeur and driven to the Indian compound. Here I had twenty NCOs – very smart – all speaking perfect English and of mixed religions. Some were Sikhs and some were Gurkhas and the competition between the two groups was very strong. Each was trying to outdo the other in all military aspects like their keenness to learn – being extremely tidy and neat and disciplined. It was an example to all, and all this because of two groups competing with one another. It was a great pleasure to be part of this training scheme and became a most enjoyable period.

About this time the desert warfare was going reasonably well. Wavell was the Commander of the desert forces and Rommel had not yet appeared on the scene, but further rumblings were coming from Europe and it looked as though Greece was on Hitler's agenda and, because of our relationship with the Greek royal families, Britain felt it was necessary to give her some military help and this was to be done by sending a brigade of British, New Zealand and Australian troops to assist in the defence of Greece.

My battalion was to be part of this and I had the responsibility of transporting all our light vehicles – scout cars, and Bren gun carriers over there. We embarked at Alexandria on the *Thurlong Castle*. She took three days to get there and we disembarked at Piraeus. We unloaded all the vehicles and awaited the arrival of the main force three days later. At this time Greece was not officially at war with the Germans so the German Ambassador was still in residence in Athens and nobody could stop him visiting the area to take stock of the arms that we had. This seemed rather stupid as no doubt he would be passing all this on to the German army. Once we had regrouped we then set about convoying the men to the Yugoslav border – I think the name of the place was Volus. We started digging trenches and setting up battle positions. The weather was bitterly cold and coming straight from the desert did not help us one bit. We were back to winter clothing. The open terrain allowed both the Germans and us to see what each was doing. We sent out listening patrols at night and were watching one another by day, and after four days in the trenches the Germans decided to attack.

Apart from the brigade of Allied troops we only had a Greek and Yugoslav contingent and the Germans took the Greek lines to attack, knowing that this was our weakest link and they had no trouble in breaking through the defences. Once they got through we knew we could be cut off so it meant we had to retreat very quickly. I had to take my section to protect the Sappers who were now blowing up our heavy equipment because we had no time to take it with us.

I had developed bad feet and both my big toes were poisoned and I could not get treatment for them. My poisoned toes were caused by having to wear boots all the time, not being able to remove them to change socks, and being one of the last to leave the front because of the job we were doing. It meant that we had to jump on the nearest vehicle available. I was able to jump on to a gun trailer with shells dropping everywhere. The tragedy of this was that we had to destroy most of our heavy arms without a shot being fired by us and the exercise seemed so futile. We now realised that the Brigade sent to Greece was no match for the German army and it all seemed a waste of time, equipment and money.

However our own job was now to retreat as quickly as possible. I was at the moment with a New Zealand company and stayed with them for

The Eastern Mediterranean
0
100
200
km
JUGOSLAVIA
SOFIA
BULGARIA
Skopje
TIRANA
R. Vardar
R. Struma
ALBANIA
Monastir
Pogradec
Florina
Vevi
Edessa
Koritza
Ptolemais
Kastoria
Kozani
MACEDONIA
R. Nestos
THRACE
Salonika
Servia
Katerini
R. Aliukmon
Mt. Olympus
Corfu
Larissa
G R E E C E
Lamia
Thermopylae
Missolonghi
Naupaktos
Euboea
Khalkis
Patras
PELOPONNESE
Megara
ATHENS
Corinth
Rafina
Piraeus
Porto Rafti
Argos
Myli
Nauplion
C. Sounion
Kalamata
N
AEGEAN SEA
Naxos
Monemvasia
Milos
C. Matapan
Kithira
Santorini
Antikithira
Canea
Kastelli Kissamou
Suda
Skarpanto
Heraklion
Sphakia
CRETE
Kasos
Hierapetra

some days as they were trying to locate the King's Royal Rifle Corps for me but, because of the retreat through Greece, it was impossible to get their exact position. We continued to retire in convoy through the centre of Greece, passing through Thebes.

While we were travelling in convoy we had to have one man on top of the truck looking for German planes straffing us and every time we heard a banging on the roof of the truck we stopped and ran to the fields. We had no time so we just had to take what was coming and hope for the best. On one occasion I ran to a field and threw myself onto the ground only to find a stream of bullets coming towards me. By sheer luck they passed so close that I was splattered with mud from the machine gun fire. The New Zealanders in my truck were on some sort of detention so they had no rifles. I had the only loaded rifle and, on the next attack by German planes, one of the New Zealanders who had fortified himself with some Greek wine decided that he would have a go with my rifle. We all ran for cover but this particular Kiwi pulled my rifle from the roof of the truck and started to fire at the enemy plane. The result was that he had a bullet pass through the cheek of his backside. I might tell you, he sobered up very quickly.

It was not long after that I was able to meet up with my Regiment and, after an investigation as to how I became detached from my unit, I was able to rejoin my Company. From here we made our way to the coast on the Aegean Sea, south of Athens, where we were to be picked up by a naval destroyer, HMS *Havock*. Having arrived on the beaches we had to set about putting all the vehicles out of action. At one time we were being attacked by Stukas. These planes only carry two or three light bombs and are able to dive at tremendous speed, pulling out at the last moment and releasing their bombs. On one of these occasions we saw this plane diving towards us and I dived for cover alongside a three-foot wall. The Stuka did his dive and it looked as if it could not miss. However, the bombs dropped the other side of the wall and we were showered by fragments from the wall. By this time I was sure I had a charmed life – the chap alongside of me pulled a packet of cigarettes from his pocket and took several long puffs. I looked at him and asked him for one. This was the first cigarette I had ever smoked, and I inhaled it as if I had always been a regular smoker. This was my introduction to smoking, which I never stopped for many years.

In the early hours of the morning we were taken off by small boats to the destroyer. We had to move quickly so that the evacuation could be completed while it was still dark, and also the Germans were very close at hand. Once aboard the destroyer we sailed through the Aegean Sea to the island of Crete. We were told that we were to be taken straight back to Egypt but because of the troops stranded on the beaches of Greece the destroyer dropped us off at Crete so that it could return to pick up some more troops. This was a Dunkirk but on a smaller scale.

An incident I would like to relate while writing about the evacuation from Greece to Crete by the *Havock* which I consider is a most surprising happening after a period of fifty years.

Recently I was visiting my son Peter, who is a New Zealander and is engaged to a young English girl, whose mother is a relation of Albert Goodey who was a stoker on the destroyer *Havock* and one evening I was talking about writing this book and mentioned the *Havock*. One thing led to another and a meeting with Albert Goodey was arranged for me. At the time of the evacuation of Greece I was taken to the boiler room to rest and was given a hot drink. Here I stayed until we reached Crete fifteen hours later. Albert Goodey and myself are almost certain that we met during this period. You can imagine we had plenty to talk about. Another surprising coincidence is that Albert's son David only lives one minute from my son's place at Nounsley, Hatfield Peverick, in Essex, so once again there were plenty of historical matters to discuss. David has spent several years researching the life of the *Havock* and I found this most interesting. I noted that some time after the fall of Crete the *Havock* ran aground on the North African coast near Libya. Two of the crew were killed and the rest of the crew were taken prisoners. Fortunately Albert Goodey had been transferred to another ship prior to this and lived to fight another day.

I find this most amazing that I should travel from New Zealand 13,000 miles away to meet this man fifty years later.

We were able to rest up on this beautiful island of Crete and recover a little from our wounds hoping that we would eventually be taken back to Egypt. It was at this time Crete was preparing for an attack by the Germans once they had taken Greece. General Freyberg was in charge of the defence of Crete and decided that we would be staying as we were the only troops that had been in combat with the Germans; Crete had nothing except ack-ack guns and small arms. We had no air force and our battalion was now reduced to an infantry unit and Crete was too far away from Egypt to be defended by fighter planes. We were now in the very early part of 1941, the weather was very nice and we were able to regroup and await the coming German attack. This, once again, was a futile effort because there was no way we were going to be able to stop the invasion of Crete and all we could do was to wait and be prepared when this started. The Germans were well-organised – first they sent over reconnoitre planes to locate the air defences. This was started in the first week in May. Having done this they sent over gliders which circled the ack-ack units. They would wait for the Stukas to attack these units. These planes were used because they could dive under the umbrella of the ack-ack fire. Once the Stukas did this the long-range guns were useless and the unit only had Vickers machine-guns to defend themselves. As the bombs were dropped everybody had to dash for the trench shelters. Once the men were in the shelter the glider crew would come in and throw grenades into the trenches. In most cases the whole unit was killed.

The glider pilots then set about destroying the guns by sealing the breeches with acid. It did not take long to silence the whole island leaving us to the mercy of the German airforce and parachute army. The glider troops would disperse into the olive groves and take up sniping. Some were captured and the others had to wait for the coming of the Germans until they had complete control. About 15th May the attack started. There were three main airstrips on the island and their objective was to attack these areas with parachutists. We were well aware that this was their next move so we set about putting up what defence we had. This was done setting up as much machine-gun fire as possible awaiting

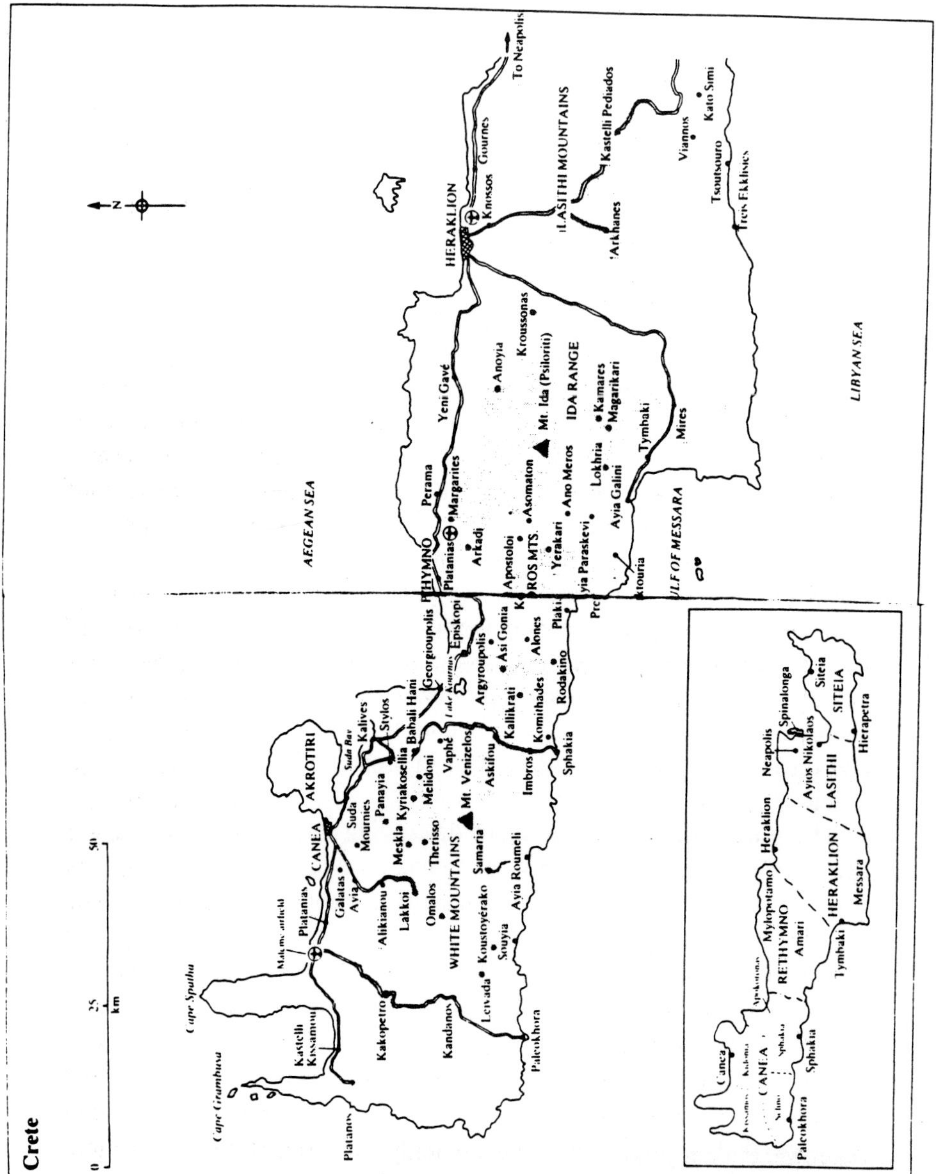
Crete
0
25
50
km
AEGEAN SEA
LIBYAN SEA
Cape Grambusa
Cape Spatha
Platanos
Kastelli Kissamou
Kakopetro
Kandanos
Paleokhora
Platanias
Galatas
Ayia
Alikianou
Lakkoi
Omalos
WHITE MOUNTAINS
Koustoyérako
Souyia
Samaria
Ayia Roumeli
CANEA
AKROTIRI
Suda
Mournies
Meskla
Therisso
Panayia
Kyriakosellia
Melidoni
Mt. Venizelos
Askifou
Imbros
Sphakia
Vaphé
Bahali Hani
Stylos
Kalives
Kallikrati
Komithades
Rodakino
Argyroupolis
Asi Gonia
Alones
Plaki
Georgioupolis
Episkopi
Platanias
Margarites
Arkadi
Perama
Yeni Gavé
Apostoloi
Yerakari
Asomaton
Ano Meros
Mt. Ida (Psiloriti)
IDA RANGE
Anoyia
Kroussonas
Lokhria
Ayia Galini
Kamares
Magarikari
Tymbaki
Mires
HERAKLION
Knossos
Gournes
To Neapolis
LASITHI MOUNTAINS
Arkhanes
Kastelli Pediados
Viannos
Kato Simi
Tsoutsouro
Tres Ekklisies
Canea
CANEA
Paleokhora
Sphakia
RETHYMNO
Mylopotamo
Amari
Tymbaki
Heraklion
HERAKLION
Messara
Neapolis
Spinalonga
Ayios Nikolaos
LASITHI
SITEIA
Siteia
Hierapetra

the attack. We knew that we were to be attacked by parachutists but did not realise that a crack unit from the German air division was to be used and from what I understand these parachutists were to be used in the invasion of England at a later date. When the final attack came we were ready. Hundreds of parachutists dropped over the airstrip, all heavily armed with machine-guns and grenades and, as they came down, they were an easy target for us and on this attack 85 per cent were killed or taken prisoner. For a while it looked as though we had the upper hand. Several attacks were made with the same result. We were able to find the signal to the planes in the air that the airstrip had been taken. Once this was done transport planes could land packed with ground troops.

We were able to fool the Germans on one occasion and they sent in their transport planes packed with troops. These planes were designed so that the sides would open thus enabling the troops to disembark easily. No sooner had they started to leave the planes when we opened up with machine-gun fire. At this stage of the operation one could say we had the upper hand – very few losses in manpower and thousands of enemy killed, and if any credit came out of the Crete operation it was that the Germans would not be able to use these parachutists in the invasion of Britain. However, the position in Crete was not to last as we were outnumbered and the eventual landing of German troops by sea took its toll. The enemy was able to set up a frontal attack and now being overwhelmed we carried out the operation of retreating. This seemed to be the only thing we did well right through Greece and Crete. Things got so bad that each section had to make its own way to an area at Canea. I took my section and we climbed a hill to reach the port of Suda Bay. At the base of this hill in an open field there was a farm house and we made our way to this house hoping that we could rest for a while. On arrival we found the house empty. We entered looking for food and drink and found some tea and rum and were able to make some tea well spliced with rum. While this was happening a German patrol had set up a machine-gun aimed at the house. They must have seen us going in and by the time we had filled our water-bottles with rum and tea, the gun raked the building and we were very quickly out of our place of protection.

On inspection of the hill I noticed a lot of boulders that would give us protection; so the idea was to all leave the house at the same time and go in different directions so as to widen the target. I gave instructions for each to make for a different boulder. This seemed to work well but I must have been the one in the sights of the machine-gun as every time I made a move to the next boulder I was shot at. I would take a good swig of the fortified tea each time I reached some shelter. I'm sure I could feel the bullets whizzing past my legs as I ran.

By this time, although I had the rum to fortify me, I was pretty exhausted and when I reached the last boulder with one more run to go I threw up my arms and dropped my rifle to the ground in an attempt to throw the Germans off guard indicating that I had been shot. This must have worked, as being absolutely exhausted, I just walked over the top of the hill without another shot being fired. How I got over the hill I will never know. I certainly had a charmed life. When I arrived over the side it was good to see that we had all escaped unhurt.

Having arrived at the port of Suda Bay we were not sure as to what we should do; so we made up our minds pretty quickly as the Germans were not far behind. On looking around the port we saw what looked like a large sailing boat anchored in the middle of the stream. We found a small rowing boat and rowed out to this ship. We found that it was a motorised ship, and by good fortune we had the sense to tie the small boat behind. There was no food on board but plenty of drinking water. We hoped that we could somehow get this ship out to sea. The Germans were now at the port and firing was going on all around us. The anchor had to be weighed by hand and the noise of the ratchet clanging echoed around the hills so much so that we had to work this every time there was a burst of gunfire. As you would realise, this took a long time, so by the time we had the anchor up, the tide had gone out and the ship was grounded – this was late in the evening and we knew that by the time morning came we would have the Germans on to us, so we had no choice but to take the rowing boat with what water we had. This boat took the whole eight of us (which was the whole section) and we had four oars, so we took it in half-hour stints to get the boat out to sea, rowing in complete darkness. Every now and then a burst of gunfire was aimed in our direction.

We realized by now that we could never have got the yacht out to sea as there were booms right across the harbour at about 200-yard intervals. Every time we approached one of these booms it meant four of us getting into the water to assist the boat over it. The rowers were getting very tired as the tide was moving in and we were rowing against it; also our hands were beginning to blister. We had been rowing for about ten hours, covering what I estimated to be eight to ten miles, when we reached the opening to the ocean but we were all too exhausted to go any further. Our hands were now covered in blisters so it was necessary we pulled ashore for some rest. We did hope to get out to the Mediterranean to get picked up by our own navy. Perhaps a little optimistic, but we had to hang on to every possibility. We came to a small inlet on the right of the coast and this was where we would rest up. When we got there we found it was thick with burnt oil from sunken ships and being so weak with exhaustion it seemed like eternity rowing that last few metres. We did get to the beach and just lay there and fell asleep. This would have been the first time we had closed our eyes in four days. By this time we were well away from the Germans. The heat of the day soon awakened us. This was 25th May and the weather was very warm.

A local Cretan passed us with a sack containing English corned beef and he gave us two tins. At the same time he indicated that a local resident just down the road spoke English and could help us. We proceeded to this farmhouse and sure enough this man could speak English having been in the USA for some years. He fed us and allowed us to rest up and was able to tell us where the Germans were and that allied forces were being evacuated from a place called Spakia. This meant we had to trek over the mountains, covering about forty miles. He also said that we would have to pass through German lines and offered to guide us over the mountains but could only take us so far. We all realised the risk this man took as he would have been shot if caught by the Germans. We accepted this generous offer of help and we had nothing to offer back other than our most humble thanks. We went with our guide as far as we could; he then indicated which direction we were to take and left us.

It was now dead of night and over the next few hours we made our way through the German lines, catching up with retreating allies. The main objective was to hold up the Germans to allow as many troops as possible to evacuate. Having arrived back with our own troops we were in the situation where we had to force march. This meant marching for fifty minutes and resting for ten minutes. However, we arrived in Spakia next day at noon. Spakia is a very rugged village on the tip of Crete facing the Mediterranean, and all the troops, which consisted of British, New Zealand and Australian, were able to hole up in a ravine facing the sea.

It was now 31st May and General Freyberg had left that morning on a Sunderland flying boat leaving General Charrington in charge. There was one ship which was to be the last to leave for Egypt that day and one in eight was to have the chance to be on it. Although this was done by ballot our section decided that only the injured men should have the chance of leaving. This left about 3,000 troops that were going to be taken prisoners of war. There was no other avenue of escape. Up to this time we were protected by the ravine in which we were hiding. On the 1st June we were told that Churchill had capitulated the island at 6 a.m. that morning, so there was nothing to do but wait for the Germans to come. We had no arms or ammunition to fight with as a few days before these had been previously given to the Marines who were to take up a rearguard position. That morning the Germans arrived and General Charrington surrendered all the troops on the island. About 10 a.m. on 1st June we were ordered out of the ravine onto the plateau with instructions to have our hands up holding a piece of white cloth. It was a beautiful day and approximately 3,000 prisoners were herded together surrounded by German machine-guns. At 10.30 a.m. two German fighter planes came out of the sky straffing us for what seemed an eternity, but took only five minutes to leave dozens of prisoners killed and hundreds wounded. We just sat there, completely shocked. With nowhere to run, once again, I must have a charmed life. We were allowed to take the injured to a local church. Those who were left were gathered and made to start marching back across Crete to Canea. At the time of the air attack I was sitting alongside of one of my fellow NCOs and we discovered that our fathers were both NCOs in the same regiment, the King's Royal Rifle Corps, before the War and I said to him with tears in my eyes, 'God, wouldn't our fathers be proud of us now.' It was a terrible experience – one I will never forget – every second is very vivid in my memory – no, I did not feel proud; I felt ashamed I had been forced into a position where I could not retaliate.

CHAPTER FOUR

We were mustered together to start the march back to Canea. I cannot remember when we last ate and there was no indication as to where the next meal was coming from. We were told we would get food if we kept walking. On one occasion we did get a small portion of rolled oats. Water was our main problem as the weather was very hot. If we saw a broken-down truck we would drain the radiator; sometimes we would come across a disused well and we would lower a can on some string. Most of the times the water was stagnant. The journey took us two days, passing through areas where fighting had taken place, passing bodies in the firing position which had been there for some days. Eventually, we arrived in Canea where we were put on the beaches. Fortunately now the weather was still good and sleeping on the beaches was no problem. At least we were able to bathe in the sea and cleanse ourselves for the first time in many days.

We were held there for three days awaiting a ship to take us back to Greece. During this time we were made to work. Most of the prisoners were taken to the airfields to bury the dead. The whole area stank of dead bodies. Fortunately, I was sent to the port with a group to unload food such as sugar, rice and currants. Sometimes we would come across a broken box of currants or an opened sack of rice or sugar and to get some back to the beach we cut a sleeve off our shirts, tied one end with a piece of string and filled it up with an assortment of these foods. We would then place it in our trouser leg so that it was not detected. On getting back to the beach we would set about making a fire to cook a concoction of rice, sugar and currants. Unfortunately, I was not able to fully cook my rice and I ate a large portion of what I thought was cooked. This swelled in my stomach and made me very ill, and I lost the lot in one way or the other.

Quite a lot of Italian prisoners were taken during the period that the British recaptured the island from them, and the Germans set them all free to loot and rape the villagers. It was horrifying to hear the screams of women being beaten and raped. The Germans seemed to enjoy this even though they didn't have much regard for the Italians. We were very distressed by our helplessness at this time as we held the people of Crete in very high regard. They were a very loving people and did not deserve the treatment that was being meted out to them – after all it was not their war.

We were on the beaches at Canea for four days waiting for a ship to take us back to the mainland of Greece. Finally, we were taken to the port where we boarded an Italian coal bunker. I can only describe this ship as I saw it. It was most probably the oldest coal bunker floating; the drive shaft was overhead allowing for a maximum of three bunkers below for the purpose of transporting coal and similar goods. The Germans gave us a ration of half a loaf of black bread and some imitation cheese and then placed 1,000 of us in each bunker. This was done by a vertical ladder which was lowered into the bunker. The only ventilation was the outlet from which we were lowered, and we were packed so tight that we could only sit and were not able to lie down. This journey took five days through the Aegean Sea to Salonika. We were in darkness except for the light from the top of the bunker. We were situated below sea level and if we had been attacked by our own navy we would have had no chance of surviving. I think this would be the only time we prayed that the Italian escort ship could protect us from our own navy.

We did survive this trip, very hungry and thirsty. The Germans used to have their fun by throwing slices of black bread down the hold and watching us fight for a piece. It was so degrading to have to survive under these conditions. Apart from being dirty from lack of water we were now breeding lice and our bodies were covered in these giving us no peace.

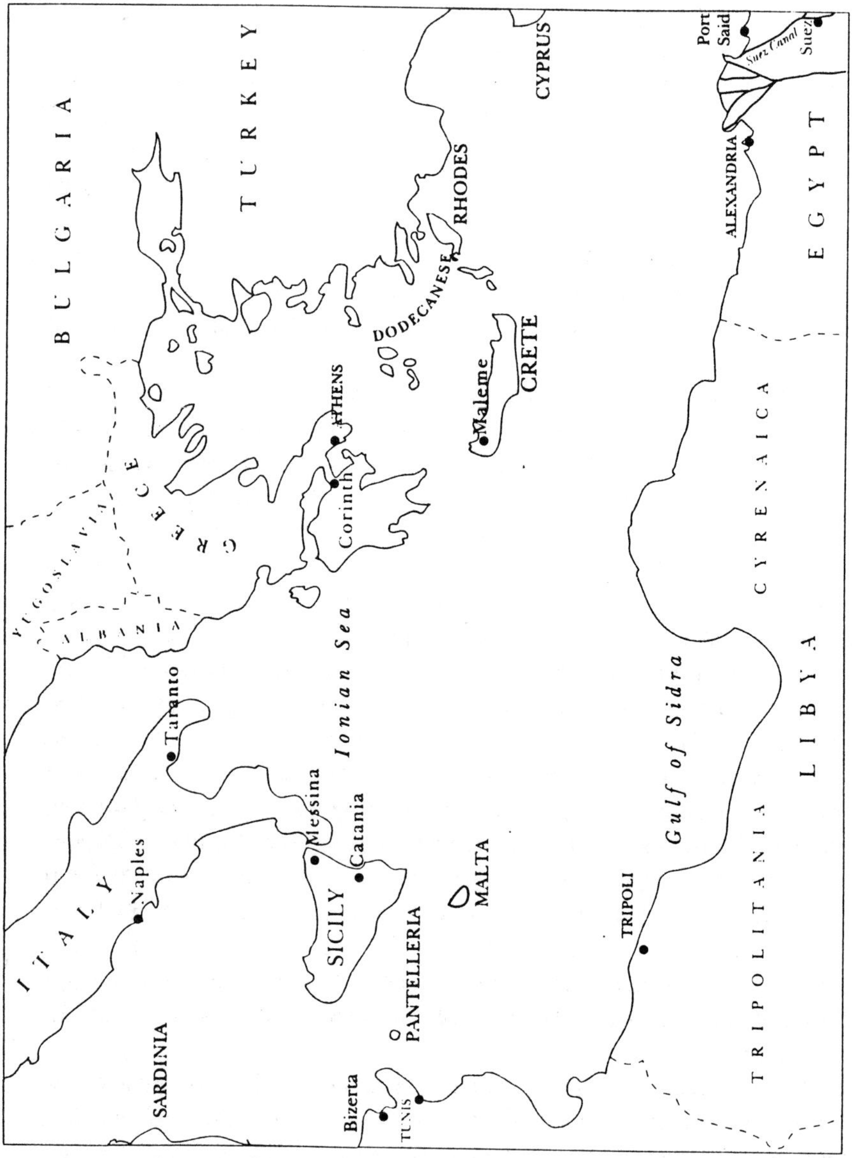

Crete and the Eastern Mediterranean. In 1941 Malta, Crete and Cyprus were garrisoned by British troops.

On arrival at Salonika we were marched to a POW camp; this again was a frightening experience. We did get some watered cabbage soup which kept us going but at this stage food did not seem important, surviving was. You felt you could get your throat cut any day as some of these men from different parts of Europe looked really menacing. However, we were only there for a couple of days when all Crete POWs were moved to the railway station for transportation to Germany. Here we were put into freight or cattle trucks, about thirty-five to a truck, and once again given a half loaf of black bread with the German ersatz cheese. This had to last us until we reached Austria. We were given an open bucket as our toilet. Protecting what little food we had was a problem; we could trust no one. Your own men would creep up and steal what little food you had. In my case my piece of bread was strapped to my stomach, so if I slept I would awaken. I think this could be described as the lowest ebb of one's life. In fact, we were worse off than rats, living in our own mess and lice ridden.

Our journey took us through Yugoslavia, Bulgaria and then into Austria. This was a slow trip as we always had to make way for military trains, and this meant pulling into sidings to allow them to pass. When we reached Belgrade the Red Cross was able to issue us with one arrowroot biscuit each. I will never forget this as they most likely saved our lives. Unfortunately, I broke my dental upper plate on these and had to survive the next four years with half a denture. Sometime later the train pulled into a siding to allow us to stretch our legs and get some fresh air. This was on a railway line in some country field so there was no chance of escaping. As it was very hot we took our clothes off and laid them out in the sun, and the lice crawled out in their hundreds. Sometimes we would use a pointed stick to scrape the lice out. At this time some of the lice were breeding under the skin. Every time they bit they drew blood. After two or three hours we were back in the trucks locked up for the rest of the journey.

After several days we arrived at Mooseburg which was Stalag 7A. This was a transit camp for labour camps all over Austria and Southern Germany. On arrival we were taken to a de-lousing centre. Firstly, we all had a shower – the first for weeks. Our clothes were put into a gas chamber to kill the lice and then we were taken to have all our hair shaven from our bodies. One minute we all had large mops of hair, and the next everybody was bald. Our greatest worry was if the hair was going to grow by the end of the War.

Little did we know that we were going to be prisoners of war for the next four years. We were taken to large huts which took over 300 prisoners. These had three-tier bunks. We were given a hot meal of cabbage and potato soup. The thought of going to bed in blankets, nice and clean, seemed like a complete luxury. Once we were in bed we found our next problem. Hoppy fleas! These fleas could hop about two feet in the air. They would bite you and hop away. With the lice you could catch them as they bit you but these jokers were well away before you had a chance, and there were so many it was a hopeless task. When you looked at the ground outside you could see these fleas jumping everywhere. However, as this was a transit camp it was not long before we were sent to a labour camp. At this camp there was no recognition of the Geneva Convention. In 1941 we had no German prisoners of war, so the German military could do what they liked and as a Warrant Officer I was compelled to work in the labour camp. By this time I had been separated from my section and was destined for a labour camp in the West End Strause of Munich. Our job was to extend the Munich marshalling yards. We were collected at 4.30 a.m. and after a cup of coffee and some bread and cheese were marched for one and a half hours to the marshalling yards. There we worked for eleven hours plus one hour's rest for food. At this time the weather was freezing. All work had to be done with shovels; no other tools were available other than an iron mallet. It was so cold that the metal rails would stick to our hands. At six o'clock we finished work and were marched back to the camp where we got a hot meal. The food was never enough and we were always hungry. Some of us used to watch the German guards eating to see if they left anything. The Germans used to leave something on purpose so they could watch the prisoners rush for the food. They seemed to get a lot of enjoyment out of humiliating the prisoners. At this time the Red Cross parcels began to arrive so we were able to get a more balanced diet. These parcels contained at least twelve items together with a tin of cigarettes.

The idea was to try and give one parcel to each prisoner of war per week but it very rarely worked this way. Sometimes there was only one parcel between four or six people. If any of us went sick we still had to do camp duties like cleaning, peeling potatoes, storing potatoes in the ground or boot repairing. We always tried to create a festive atmosphere and I can remember our first Christmas. The hut we were in held thirty-five prisoners and we had a corner of the room where we made tea and converged to play cards, chess, etc. On Christmas Day we tried to create the Christmas spirit. We made decorations with cigarette packets, and imitation cakes made of bread so the table gave the impression of the real thing. Beer bottles with weak beer, which the Germans supplied us with, were saved for this day. Parts of our Red Cross parcels were also for this occasion. On Christmas Day German officers came to look at our festive table and took photos as propaganda to show how well they were looking after the POWs. As the room leader, I was questioned regarding the table, and they got round to asking me what I thought of the German food. I told them it was rubbish only fit for pigs, but they said, 'Your own men do the cooking.' I replied that since they gave them a large vat and just cabbage and potatoes, how could they expect them to cook a decent meal. I felt quite good about my reply to the officers until I found out that they had been back to the chaps that were doing the cooking and told them that I said they were not cooks. I was now No.1 enemy of the cooks and it was not until some time later, with a room-mate, that we were able to put matters right with the cooks and tell them what actually happened.

It was about this time that the Germans found out that I had experience in cooking and the next morning the camp interpreter told me that I was to report to the Germans' cookhouse to cook for the German guards. I realised I had a problem. All sorts of things could happen if I refused. They could transfer me to the salt mines or I could be accused of assisting the enemy. After discussion with one or two of my seniors I decided to go to the cookhouse but would do it my own way and on this particular day I had a meat roll, potatoes, cabbage and onions. I cooked the meat in batter, well fried the onions, made mashed potatoes and cabbage more like the English way of eating. The Germans do not like food cooked this way. They like sauerkraut and did not like the battered meat roll and hardly ate any of the food I prepared. I was accused of trying to poison the guards and the medical officer came down to check the food. Fortunately, this officer had spent some time in England and spoke perfect English. He sat down to a meal which I prepared for him and ate most of it and said there was nothing wrong with the food except that Germans did not like this style of cooking. I said I only knew the English way of cooking and should not have been sent there in the first place. This worked well and I was relieved from working in the German cookhouse. Thank goodness! The last thing I wanted to be accused of was that I was working for the Germans.

It was about this time I was getting restless and realised that we were going to be there a long time, so I started to think of a plan with the possibility of either getting to England or Switzerland. I had a talk with one of my friends, who incidentally came from my home town. His name is Robert Towsey and we decided to look at the possibility of getting away. At this stage of POW life there were no escape committees from which to get help. We listed the things we would have to take with us, such as clothing, hats, compass and food. The latter was a problem as we had so little food already, but with care we could save a little each time we received a parcel. We knew it would take at least three months to prepare a way of getting out of the camp. This would require tools to cut the barbed wire and I did this by getting work in the shoe shop where we repaired boots for the prisoners. In this job I was able to take hammers and pliers for cutting the wire. The route we were going to take was across Munich, over the River Isar, on to the Brenner Pass and then into Switzerland. I had a rice paper air force map which I was able to reprint on photographic paper. This gave me a negative print of the area which was cut into playing-card size and numbered so that we could handle whatever part of the map we required. After use it could be torn up into small pieces and discarded. This plan did work quite well.

Clothes were no problem. It was easy to bribe the civilians with cigarettes or chocolate to get what you wanted. In the shoe shop I was able to make hollow heels in my boots to conceal German money if we were caught. This was another good plan because we did have to use this money. All this preparation took just over three months. Autumn was getting nearer so it was necessary to put the plan into operation. Before this we had to plan the escape from the camp.

Alongside the labour camp was a small hospital and the plan was to leave the camp from the hospital. We had air-raid shelters around the camp and one of these crossed into the hospital separated by barbed wire. We estimated it would take us one hour to cut through both lots so it was necessary to leave the camp by 5 p.m. to get across to Munich and over the River Isar before the curfew at 8 p.m. The camp had a guard patrol and we had several friends who set up a signal to let us know when the guards were turning the corner. Apart from cutting the wire, we estimated that we could be free of the camp in just over an hour, but we had one problem. Every night a guard would visit the hut to ensure that all were present. His name was Schultz and he came from Austria. He used to sit on my bed and we would have a chat. He could see no sense in the War and was one of the nicer type of German. After a chat he would go on his way so I had to break this pattern. When he came into the room each night I would be in another part of the hut and would get rid of him without him being suspicious. On the day of our departure I made a dummy in the bed.

We had done our homework and it was now the middle of September, so we decided that it was time to go. At 4 p.m. on this particular day we put on our civvy clothes and Austrian hat. The first cutting of the wire was easy as this was done in the air-raid shelter. Once through the barbed wire we were in the hospital grounds. Now we had to work in the open with guards patrolling. To cut the wire we had to hold the pliers gripped over the wire and hit them with the hammer. The idea was to cut a gate so that when we got through our lookout could replace the wire and, hopefully, the guards would not notice this.

The cutting of the gate took longer than expected. The delay when the guards were turning the corner also took longer than we thought. However, having done all the damage, there was no turning back, so we signalled to our lookouts that we were going the next time the guards turned the corner. The first move was to open the barbed-wire gate we had cut, knock down the palings of a fence and run as fast as we could across a 200 yard field to the roadway. All this had to be done before the guards reappeared. Also our lookout had to replace the palings and put the wire fence back so that nothing amiss would be noticed. This part of the operation went well. We had one scare after being out for only five minutes. One of the German cooks who was also in civilian clothes was walking toward us.

As we passed I nodded and said 'good night' in German and he replied back with 'gute nacht'. We were well-pleased about this as we had got past him unrecognised in our civilian clothes. At this stage we knew that we would not get across the River Isar before the curfew so we decided to go to the marshalling yards where we had been working and hide up in one of the lofts in the building that stored the fish plates and sleepers. It was now beginning to get dark, so we hurried and arrived at the yards in good time. It was a simple job getting into the shed and up into the loft and here we would have to stay until about 5 p.m. next day until the prisoners had left. We made ourselves comfortable and had some sleep. We could make some tea by using a methylated tablet. This was lit and put in something that you could stand a mug on and heat your water.

The ceiling of the building was made of 12" x 1" planks and we could see all that was going on below. The next morning the prisoners arrived and started work and every now and then someone would come into the shed for some materials. Little did they know that we were in the ceiling watching them.

Everything went well that day – as soon as the prisoners stopped work to return to camp we came down from our hiding place and mixed with the crowds. We had to walk right across Munich and felt quite confident that so far we had done our job well. We crossed the River Isar just before dusk and kept walking all night. We discovered some days later that we had been found missing at eight o'clock on the day we escaped. Old Schultz, the friendly guard had found the dummy in my bed so the search was out all over the area. Little did they know that we were only a few miles away that evening.

It was the plan whilst on this escape to walk through the big towns during the day and the small villages at night. In large towns you can mingle with the crowds unnoticed, and in the villages you would be easily noticed if you passed through them during the day. This plan was working well up to the moment. We kept to the woods and only travelled on the roads when passing through a town. After two days we were running out of water and having our army uniforms on under our civvies made us perspire so no water became a problem. At the next farm I left Bob, my partner, in the woods and walked into the farmyard, passing a farmhand with a polite 'gute morgan', filled my two water bottles and returned to the woods where we both had a good long drink.

On the third day we were approaching a town we thought was called Holtzkirchen. On our map this looked like a large town but as we neared it we could see it was only a small village. The reason it was given prominence on the map was that it was the centre of the timber yards so we were misled into thinking this was a large town. We had no option then but to keep on walking. It was exactly 12 noon that we crossed the main street. As we crossed going south a local policeman passed going eastward. We kept walking, not looking back to arouse suspicion but after going about 500 yards out of the village this policeman pulled up on his cycle and for half an hour we tried to explain we were labour workers returning from holiday to our place of work. We almost got away with this but could not produce any papers of identification so he asked us to return to the police station to prove that we were conscript workers. Here we had to decide what to do. We could overpower this policeman and make a run for it or go back to the station. It is a rule that you never commit a civilian crime because you would be tried by a civilian court and you never know what the outcome would be; so I said to Bob, 'Let's go back. If we give ourselves up we will at least have a chance to have another go at escaping.'

On our return to the station we realised that the game was up, so we finally told the policeman that we were British soldiers and had escaped from Munich. They did not know what to believe and they spent the next hour contacting all the local workers' camps to check whether or not they had any missing workers. As they could not get any results the officer decided to ring Munich and it was confirmed that we were the two prisoners they had missing. We were taken to the police cells awaiting a guard to take us back to Munich. The cell had two bunks with one high iron bar window. I climbed on Bob's back and looked down on some very hostile locals who had come to know that two British soldiers were in the prison. They were throwing anything they had to hand at the window. It was obvious that they had a lot of hatred for the British and we thought that we were in the safest place at that time.

On being recaptured we had plenty of food, chocolate and cigarettes. We knew we had to feed ourselves well in preparation for the punishment to come. Apart from this we were able to do some bartering with the two local policemen. As I have said before, a bar of soap and chocolate worked wonders and we could exchange these for local hot food, so by the time the guard came from Munich to take us back all the food had been used up in one way or another.

After three days the guard arrived and we were escorted to the railway station for our journey back. The last carriage of German trains then was only used for carrying POWs and conscripted workers to and from work, so we got mixed up with some French POWs returning to camp and we were able to pass the maps and compass over to them. We were amazed that the policemen had not already taken these from us, neither did they take our food – just bartered with us for it. The only thing we had left was the German money concealed in the heel of my boot.

We were later taken back to the transit camp – Stalag 7A in Austria. We arrived there late that evening and were taken to a room to be searched. They asked us what we had done with maps, etc., and we told them that the local police had taken them. When they took my boots they did everything except tear them apart but eventually gave them back to me with the money still concealed. This money came in handy to use as bribes when we were placed in confinement. We were then placed in a small cell with no bed or other facilities until the morning. At about 9 a.m. next morning we were taken to a large room with maps on the wall ready for interrogation where we had to show the route we had taken and tell them why we had escaped. We told them as soldiers of the British Army it was our duty to get back and fight for our country. The officers who interrogated us spoke perfect English and had spent quite some time in England. Nevertheless, I thought he would explode when I gave him our answer. When asked how we got our clothes, maps and tools to make our escape, we told them it was very easy to bribe the civilian population with soap and chocolate. I knew that these replies were not helping us but felt we had to put up a stand against the arrogance of the officers.

After they had finished we were given three weeks on bread and water in a prison camp. All our mates had by now heard that we were back and set up a system to try and get some food to us as they knew we were in for a rough time. There were a mixed lot in the prison – about forty. Some were Russians, others were Poles and a real menacing lot. The Russians would indicate that they would like to cut Churchill's throat because he would not start a second front in France. Here again bribery came to the fore. With the money we had we were able to procure small amounts of bread to keep us going. Sometimes we got a little cheese but were very thankful with what we could get. Anyway, we survived the three weeks and on our release from confinement we were both posted to different camps. Bob Towsey was sent to the Polish border to a POW camp there and I was sent to a camp just outside Nuremburg. This camp was called Oflag 3 C but later changed to Stalag 383. I never saw Bob Towsey again until after the War. He is still alive and lives in Barking, Essex, and whenever I take a trip back to England we meet and have a talk about old times.

The camp I was sent to was a new camp made up of warrant officers and would eventually hold 6,000 prisoners of war. It was situated in a German military zone which made it impossible to escape from although many more tried.

Room 104 in Company 1 was where I was to spend the next three years as a POW. Stalag 383 was situated in Hohenfels in the Bavarian Valley approximately 90 miles from Munich. For four months of the year everything is frozen. Icicles are all around the hut and the snow that gets into the huts remains frozen. You dressed when you went to bed in the heaviest woollen clothes you could find – balaclavas and mittens included. When you went to the wash-house the walls were coated with at least a foot of ice and this is where we would shower winter and summer. When wood was available from our forest labours we would have a fire for part of the day. Sometimes we were desperate for fuel. To make tea we had to contribute one of our bed boards, and of course as time went on we landed up with no bed boards with the bed being supported with string from our Red Cross parcels, and as fuel became very, very short we had to look at the hut to see which beams we could dislodge, and I'm sure that after four years had we to survive there another winter the hut would have collapsed. All through the winter the area was frozen solid with snow. Food was very short, but we did get Red Cross parcels, sometimes one a week. Sometimes it was one between three or four men. One parcel a week would just be enough to survive on, so we would be perpetually hungry. The Germans did not provide much food. Most of it was in the form of weak vegetable soup.

In each hut there were fourteen bunks and one table and a couple of forms. The fourteen NCOs were people from all walks of life; we had three Australians, four Londoners and the rest from different parts of England, and comradeship seemed to come to the fore in such difficult times. In all my time in Room 104 I cannot recall any fights or serious arguments. There was, of course, times when our patience was stretched to the limit. One amusing incident I can recall. Our toilet block was situated about 100 yards from our hut, and during the cold winter nights it was a long way to go to relieve ourselves, and to overcome the problem each one of us had the largest tin we could find and hung this on the outside of the hut with our name on the outside of the tin. These tins were for the purpose of relieving ourselves to save the treacherous walk to the toilet block. Each one of us would empty our own tin every morning. A problem would arise when someone would use another persons can to save having to empty his own next morning. Quite often you would get up only to find your can already full. The next morning discussions would develop as to who used whose can. Needless to say, we never solved the problem.

We did find it very difficult living in a confined space with fourteen people and sometimes got on one another's nerves, but all in all we managed. It was a case of having to. We had a daily roster for keeping the hut tidy and one person was delegated as head of rations. He was in charge of all food and parcels and his job was to see that all food was evenly distributed. We were able through bartering with the German guards (this was the time of the handcuff episode) to procure two rabbits – one a Belgian hare and the other an Angora rabbit. They were put together to produce a litter for the hut. It was very difficult to get enough grass to feed these. It mostly had to come from outside the compound or when we were on wood detail. They never got enough food and when they did produce some offspring they were just skeletons. The idea was to produce one rabbit a fortnight for rabbit stew. This did not last long as the Germans ordered that all rabbits be confiscated so we killed them all and ate them.

We all kept our sanity by taking up our own hobbies; playing chess, draughts, bridge and taking up some form of learning, and this went on, living in hope, never giving up, until the end of the War.

About this time, of course, quite a number of the German army were being captured as prisoners either in the desert or in other areas, also in Russia. It was now a question of the Geneva Convention being forced upon the German hierarchy as now their own troops were being captured. Life now became a little more tolerable and this camp was, as I've said, set up mainly for warrant officers and the idea was, of course, from that time on warrant officers would not have to go out and work in the labour force such as salt mines and other onerous types of duties that nobody else wanted to do. So there we were at our own devices more or less within this camp. As I mentioned before, we had 6,000 troops of all nationalities. I know there were a few Canadians there, a lot of New

Zealanders, Australians, quite a few from the Maori battalion, of course a lot of British, Welsh and Scottish, a few South Africans, everybody who was a warrant officer from the allied army. We didn't have to work. The only work that was done by these people was if they volunteered and you can rest assured that very, very few volunteered.

One of the main assets that we had with this type of camp, that all being warrant officers, we had a cross section of people in all types of education. It didn't matter whether it was painting, music, art, manual work like building carpentry, there was always somebody that was very, very good at this job and very good at training, so we were able to set up within the camp some type of education system. We were able to obtain certain kinds of books from the Red Cross where we could form a library. Books were sent out by families to various people and this helped contribute in building up a wealth of knowledge for everybody. So to pass the time away we all set up with our different hobbies and a lot of people actually re-educated themselves over the period that they were prisoners of war, and this was to everybody's advantage when they came back to civilian life. Also, it stopped the form of insanity that was creeping up on people about this stage and I suppose we were all getting a bit funny in our ways. The isolation away from civilian life, never being able to speak to a female, having to live and tolerate living with one another for twenty-four hours a day in confined spaces, and anyway as I say, we all grew to be different people by the time we left, as the War came to an end.

Education systems were set up and I know in some cases where people had sat for different degrees, it was possible that these papers could be sent by the Red Cross for them to sit their various exams and one or two people I know were very successful in obtaining their scholarships through this manner. It was amazing what we did with nothing. When I say nothing there were no tools. We weren't allowed tools because they could be used as weapons. Any tool that we had, had to be made by hand, and if you could see some of the things that were created within this camp you would be utterly amazed. I've seen model railways set up. What we did with the utilisation of the ordinary tin that contained the meat and the rations that we got through the Red Cross was amazing. I've seen sheds built of tin, overlapping each one and cutting out the seams and rolling them out and making massive great sheets of tin where we could make extra small rooms for making the still to produce our home-brews. I'll tell you more about that later. So, life settled down to a confined space and everybody had a way, or most people had a way, of passing the time with some sort of interest that they liked. In my case it was music. I tried to learn to write music and develop my skills at the piano accordion at that time. I improved my speech in German. I was no fitness freak but I knew that I had to keep myself as fit as I could under the circumstances and with regard to the nourishment that I had. Quite a number of people did this. This is how life went on in Stalag 383.

We had quite a lot of confrontation with the German Commandant. He was a man that wanted peace at any price. He didn't want confrontation or any threat of disruption within the camp. His fear was that he would be sent to the Russian front. So with a very strong liaison

Inside the hut in Stalag 383. I lived in this hut for over three years together with fourteen P.O.W.s. The room measured approximately 20ft by 15 ft.

officer on the prisoner's side, I remember this was Sergeant Major MacKenzie, a very adept man at handling the Germans and getting and squeezing out of them the maximum that he could under such difficult conditions, and he was a great man. And so, as I say, life developed this way.

Of course, the main objective and obsession with everybody was escape, and I suppose it became one of the chief hobbies in most camps in Germany and this infuriated the Germans no end. We formed an escape committee and they were quite capable men. This committee would be formed of around five or six people and, if anybody in the camp had the desire to escape and he could put forward a plan which seemed to have possibilities, the escape committee would set about finding him all the necessary things that he needed to help his escape, i.e., clothes, compasses, maps and ways and means of getting out of the camp, which I can assure you was a very difficult thing. Several attempts were made; I cannot recollect in my mind at the moment anybody from that camp being successful at getting away in the early stages. Most people were caught after four, five, six days or even a fortnight afterwards and bought back for internal punishment within the camp. It was to show the futility of trying to escape from this particular camp. It was difficult because it was right in the middle of the German manoeuvring area, and there was very, very little concealment.

One of the chief hobbies of the camp was tunnelling and there were several attempts of trying to tunnel from the various huts that people lived in, out to the outer perimeter of the camp. This could mean sometimes a tunnel of anything from between two and three hundred yards and you had to be quite an engineer to achieve this objective. You can well imagine the things that were needed. First of all, electricity was no problem. We could get electricity into the tunnels. The other was timber for the shoring up of the tunnels as they proceeded, and the method used was that once a fortnight a team of people were allowed out by the Germans into the forest to cut certain timbers, marked trees for thinning out in the forests for the purpose of supplying fuel for the huts. This might mean a walk of anything from 7, 8, 9, 10 miles into the forest and the idea was to bring back as much timber as you could, bearing in mind that the ground was completely covered in snow over the winter period and the only means of fuel that we had was the timber that we could bring back to each hut. The strongest and the fittest men went from each hut and on many occasions I went and did this. The method of being able to bring back as much timber as you could was to get the longest narrow trees you could, and pile the thick ends at one end and they tapered down. These trees could be anything from 13, 14, 15 feet long and you would bind them together with a post in the middle and put them across your shoulder. By this method you could actually drag over a tonne of timber. With the snow on the ground it was very easy to glide along the ground with it. We arrived back at the camp with all this timber and once we got into the camp we would then make over so much of this timber to, what we called, the escape committee. It would be cut up into the lengths that they required and then hidden so that the tunnelling people could use these for the purpose of shoring. There were some magnificent efforts made.

I still can't recollect anybody escaping from a tunnel but when you see the efforts put into some of these tunnels, it was really amazing. To illustrate my point to you these tunnels generally started from the middle of the hut where there was a free-standing fire. The idea was that you could move this fire to one side and start your tunnel from there, so that when you had finished for the day, or you could put the fire back in position, the Germans would not have any indication that the tunnel was in progress. You might say to yourself, well where did we get rid of the soil and the stuff that we were digging out of these tunnels. Well, this was another big problem and we had volunteers that, as the soil was being brought up from the tunnel, it was put into long socks, put down the side of our trousers and as we walked round the camp we would gradually sprinkle all the soil over the ground. We didn't have piles of dirt everywhere that you would expect to see when tunnelling. This particular tunnel I am talking about would be a good 200 yards long, and work went on for months. At 7.30 every morning everybody had to get up from their beds and go out into the main street or pathway and assemble for counting, and we all had to line up in fives. It was always a great joke that the German posturns there could only count in fives.

On this particular day we had had a lot of rain and I think it had rained for two or three days and the ground was getting quite soggy. During the course of the counting of this parade from this particular hut where the tunnelling had started, the whole thing caved in to the end of the wire of the camp, and it was a complete shock to the Germans to find that all this had been going on under their noses. Mind you it disheartened the people that were building the tunnel. This was of such great interest to the Germans that they bought several people from outside the camp to inspect what had actually taken place. Of course nobody was in the tunnel because most of the work went on at night anyway when there were no Germans about. So that was months and months of work that just went up in the air at a moment's notice but this is to try and illustrate to you the amount of enthusiasm and effort that was put in by the escape committees and volunteer workers. There were several other escape attempts, such as trying to hide people in refuse bins which in one case a couple of people got out of the camp and almost reached Vienna. I cannot recall any more such instances.

The currency in the camp at that time was the almighty cigarette. Anything that was bartered or sold depending on supply and demand, had a price tag of so many cigarettes. There used to be quite a number of stalls. I know that we had one in our hut. We used to take the door off our hut and use this as a table upon which we would display the things we had in excess. It might be a pullover or something else in our parcels that we did not require. A smoker wanted cigarettes so was quite happy to trade something from his food ration to get the almighty cigarette he wanted so badly. This developed into quite a shopping spree. As a matter of fact, it was quite interesting to get up in the morning and say we'd do a round of the stalls and see what was going. It was surprising what used to come from these stalls. The prices of the goods depended on the supply of cigarettes. If there were plenty in the camp the prices would go down. Similarly if there was a shortage the prices went up and so on and so forth. What you could buy for five cigarettes one day might cost you ten next time. It was all controlled by what we call the supply and demand system, and this went on right throughout the camp. One other pastime was producing alcohol, the main ingredients of which were potato peelings, prunes or any foodstuff that was suitable for fermenting. With a little bit of ingenuity it was quite simple to build a sealed unit and a condenser for the purpose of producing spirit. It would take a whole day to produce a small bottle of colourless, clear spirit. To test the alcohol content we would place a piece of cloth dipped in alcohol close to the fire. If it ignited readily the spirit was bottled and put away for a festive occasion. This idea caught on and there were many stills in operation throughout the camp. This developed to such a degree that many POW's got out of control drinking this spirit and were continually drunk, and many of the chaps were admitted to hospital with damaged stomachs. It became necessary for the hospital staff to ask the Germans to have all these stills destroyed. These little sheds were being made from the tin cans that I mentioned before. You can make great sheds with them and build them up and have these little stills running just outside your hut, and they had to plead with the Germans to destroy them which they attempted to do because they had so many people in the hospital with damaged stomachs. I won't mention the country, but there was one particular group of people that loved making this grog, and boy, they got themselves in a hell of a state. However, all good things came to an end and I know that this was one that wisdom in the end forced everyone to cease the operation because of the damage that it was doing.

Many people had the ability to build radios with what materials they could find in the camp and what we could bribe the Germans with. To get back to the bribery side of it I had better go back to when the Dieppe attack was made on France. I'll have to look up the date of this but it was somewhere in 1942 when Britain decided to test the French coastline by performing an invasion of France. I don't know how successful they intended to be but they did make a landing and I think most Canadian forces were involved in this. They did establish a small beachhead and, of course, they captured some Germans. Now at this stage they had no way of being able to confine these Germans into a camp situation so what they did was to put their hands behind their backs and tie their thumbs together. Now I can assure you that if you put a person's hands behind his back and tie his thumbs together it makes him completely incapable and there is nothing he can do. So this is what they did and herded them all together. The German army thought this was a very bad way of dealing with the German prisoners, so they had to retaliate in some way. As you know the invasion fizzled out, but that's another story.

The retaliation the Germans resorted to was using handcuffs and where they got them from I don't know, but they produced thousands upon thousands of them. Now these handcuffs had chains on them about 18 inches long with a handcuff on each end. As a reprisal they said they would handcuff every prisoner in Germany from 7.30 in the morning until 7.30 at night before they went to bed. I don't know where they got them from but the handcuffs duly arrived and these were handled by home-guard type of soldiers. They were men in their late forties, I suppose we were being a little bit unkind to them; we called them 'The Goons' with their German hats on and long, long grey coats right down to their ankles and jackboots on and, as I say, they weren't what you'd call front-line soldiers. They used to come in every morning, handcuff us and come along at 7.30 at night and as they thought, with their keys release us. It didn't take us long with ingenuity to make a key or get something that would quite easily undo these handcuffs, and the idea was that if you went out walking around the camp you had one handcuff on one wrist and held the other in your pocket. Then if there was a German about you immediately sort of crossed them over and just hooked it over your arm. It was farcical in many ways because it didn't put us out in any way but it created a tremendous avenue for being able to contact these Goons, as we called them, for the purpose of bartering for these things. It was quite amusing that these Germans used to arrive in each hut with their long grey coats on, and they'd come to each hut to take the handcuffs off everybody but in the end as they walked into the hut generally the handcuffs were hanging on the back of the door anyway because we'd already got them off, but the important thing was it gave access for the Germans to get amongst the prisoners to trade cigarettes, soap and chocolate and things like that. So the world in many respects was our oyster and they were quite happy to trade for a bar of soap to take home to their frau or cigarettes for themselves, which they could never get. So anything that we wanted was available to us and little bits of equipment for making radios and things like that appeared on the scene.

I was very interested in photography, as I told you. I used to make the maps for the escape committee and I needed the paper and the chemicals for the purpose of doing this and, with a few cigarettes here and there, a small bar of chocolate or a piece of soap, we were able to procure these things. To get back to the radios. Several radios were made by the people that had the ability to be able to do this, and there were quite a number. It's amazing the results they got from even some of the equipment within the camp to be able to make a radio and there would be a committee set up of say around twelve people, who contributed so much in the form of cigarettes for the purpose of bartering, and within a short space of time we had a radio. The idea was that amongst these twelve people alternately each night or evening at around about 6 o'clock when the main news came from Britain, six would come in and listen to the radio and the other six would be out as lookouts for Germans so that anything of a suspicious nature happening with regard to a German in the vicinity the whole system was taken down and hidden in a special hiding place that had been set up beforehand.

It was very nostalgic, the emotion of listening to the BBC 6 o'clock news getting an authentic up-to-date situation of what was happening because by this time things were beginning to turn our way. We had got past the *Prince of Wales* sinking and Singapore falling and so on and so forth and now the tide was beginning to turn and we were making advances in the desert. Rommel was being set back and we were gaining ascendancy of the seas and the Americans were handling the Japanese quite well. It was good news that we were getting and it did us a hell of a lot of good. We were able at the time to listen to Ann Shelton and Vera Lynn. There was a half an hour programme before the news and we could listen to both of them singing obviously for the purposes of the troops. It was very emotional and very touching, I can assure you, when you have spent so long as a prisoner of war, this was food for our resistance against the Germans.

The Germans used to deliver their own format as to how the War was going. They would collect us all out on the main arena of the camp and the Camp Commandant would tell us all how the Russian steamroller was being crushed and they were due to attack the Allies and invade England, and all sorts of things – anything to try and demoralise us because we just used to laugh at it because we could hear the authentic news for ourselves. For those that couldn't listen to it there was a type of report that was given out verbally by the different liaison officers who were set up in different companies. The whole camp was set up in different companies and this used to be relayed by these liaison officers to the various rooms so that the people who weren't fortunate enough to be able to listen to the radios could get what was happening on the front. As you can see, the morale was beginning to rise dramatically because of the way the War was going and this, as I say, continued. Every now and then, the Germans used to get a hint of where a radio was. They had many devious ways of trying to find their information.

One of the great occupations that we used to have was walking and we had a parade ground alongside the camp where we carried on our different sporting activities. Any ideas, we had thousands. Well, most of the troops would be walking round in this large circle which I would say, the outer perimeter would cover a quarter of a mile, and you would be walking and there would be mumble mumble, everybody would be talking and talking about different things and, of course, the Germans had the ability to dress a man as a prisoner and to put him in amongst the people walking around and he would understand the English, and it was amazing what they were able to collect in information. Every now and then we would find a raid on a particular hut where a radio was confiscated. Needless to say, there was always a back up; we would be able to produce another one at some time or another. This was a battle that went on with the Germans all the time. They had the battle of trying to find out what we were up to and we had contingencies where, if we lost something, we could replace it.

The Germans tried all sorts of devices to undermine our morale. They claimed that they had a British Force made up of prisoners of war, fighting on the Russian front against Communism. They also had several men who spoke excellent English arrive at Camp 383 for the purpose of enlisting men to help make up this force. We told the Commandant in no uncertain terms that if these men came into the camp they would get a very hostile reception. They did not get into the camp but I'm sure they existed. On another occasion a POW arrived in the camp claiming that he had been taken in prisoner in Italy. He looked very smart and spoke good German and set about establishing himself as a go-between for the POW's and the Germans. If the Germans deprived us of any of our equipment for certain hobbies this man would get it returned to us. This went on for some time and we really thought this chap was genuine, but all the while the Germans were swooping down on our radios, cameras and escape equipment. It was then we realised that this POW was a German sympathiser and was being used for the purpose of gathering important information which he passed on to the Germans. Once this was known that his game was up he was quickly removed to another POW camp. I understand that when the War ended he was arrested as a traitor and dealt with accordingly.

As I told you, I was interested in photography at that time and I earned myself a bit of currency in the form of cigarettes to produce photographs that people wanted. Believe it or not, I also had a camera and photographs were printed and we were able to produce what we call a censor stamp which was made out of clay and produced in such a way that it was just about similar to the German type of censor stamp that they passed their letters or photographs with. So it did turn out very successful as far as I was concerned. Apart from producing the maps for the escape committee I could set about building up an album of photographs for myself and also for people that happened to have a negative or something that they wanted reprinted. I built up quite a little bank of currency in the way of cigarettes which allowed me to barter round and get some of the things that I wanted for myself, like an extra bar of chocolate or food. Without any warning one night at about 7 o'clock two Germans descended into the hut and got everyone out of bed and they set to trying to ransack it looking obviously for this camera. Well, they found the camera, they found the papers, they found the equipment, they found everything that I had. They traced the wires around the room where they were hidden. Where they got the information from I just don't know. It could have been done by a method of slow process of listening, what they called their listening devices of putting people into the camp, walking around of a night time and listening to what people said.

It didn't deter us too much. It took us some time but we were able to get back into some kind of business although I never had a camera again. I was still able to produce things from negatives and also carry on the work for the escape committee because while the handcuff system was going on we could get exactly what we wanted. One illustration I'd like to give you. As I say, we had all sporting activities there. We had test matches against the Aussies, we had cricket matches. I was interested in the art of self-defence, not boxing for the purpose of becoming professional in the sport but mainly for the purpose of self-defence and I was quite proud of what I was able to achieve. I did enter one or two, what they called, exhibition matches in which I acquitted myself quite well, at least I thought I did. I never took it up seriously at all because it wasn't in my mind to become a boxer in any way; it was just another form of keeping myself occupied under what I call very, very difficult conditions. This escape committee thing; I got to be known quite well as regards photography.

As the War came to an end and the Germans were fast in retreat it was felt that because we were all warrant officers that there could be some reprisals on the camp. It was thought at the time that the SS could come into the camp and say try to annihilate us or shoot us up and...anything was possible. I had one of the medical officers approach me and ask me if I would print 3,500 maps of the area and they said, 'We will report you sick; we will transport you to the hospital [which was about half a kilometre away] and we will give you a room and lock you in it with all the equipment you want; we'll get the equipment for you and what we would like you to do is to produce 3,500 maps of the area.' Now this, obviously, was the purpose that if it became known that this was going to happen and that if everyone's life was at stake, everyone would be given a map of the area and it would be up to them to try to get out of the camp by mass means. So I was duly reported sick and I had from 6 o'clock one night until 6 o'clock in the morning, and I actually produced 3,500 maps in what I call black and white negative of the area of Hohenfels, which was where our camp was situated, so that if the POWs were able to get out they had a map in which to get them on the road to wherever American or British troops might be fighting.

At this time I think I am right in saying the Third and the Seventh Army were approaching the camp and nobody knew exactly how they were going to arrive. Nobody knew when they were going to arrive. We knew that they were so many miles away and there was no resistance because at this time the Germans were actually running; when I say running it was very difficult to see a German standing still. We had a few at the camp that were still controlling it and we got orders one morning to pack up all our gear and get up onto the parade ground, the big sports ground that we had, and the idea was that we were going to go out onto a forced march. Now we didn't know where we were going. We heard rumours that we were going to be held hostage somewhere but in situations like this of course rumours are rife anyway. We didn't know, but we knew we were going to be marched further into Germany and that's about all. Well, I got up into this area with all my gear and, of course, the German fighter planes were straffing the streets and straffing everything outside. They knew where the camps were, so the safest place to be at that time was in the camp because everybody was getting a bashing outside by fighter planes. We could hear Nuremberg being bombed and even Frankfurt from long distance. It occurred to me that this was something I didn't want to do. I didn't feel that my life was worth going out into those streets in a marching formation. You have got to realise that nobody could ever identify us as Allied troops because we were wearing a conglomerate of bits of old German 1940 uniforms, French uniforms, panteloons, you name it, we looked a very motley lot together with our own uniforms, our own bits of British uniforms that we had. So we looked just like a lot of refugees I suppose, and the thought of being out on these roads from high up you could look like Germans retreating or the enemy retreating and I had visions of us all being straffed to pieces not only by the Germans but also being done over by our own Air Force, so this didn't appeal to me at all.

I set about dreaming up a scheme of what I could do, as we were up on this area for quite some hours. I indicated to the German at the gate that I was leaving all my gear on the camp, I was feeling sick, I had to go to the toilet. The fact that I was leaving all my gear there I suppose he thought to himself, 'Well he's got to come back for it.' And so they let me go back down into the camp. Having got into the camp I didn't worry about my gear. I was looking at self-preservation. I thought to myself, 'Well, what is the safest way with the War coming to an end, that I could preserve my well-being.' So I went back to the hut; the whole camp was desolate. There was nobody about at all and I lifted up some of the floor boards. These floor boards were done in sections of say somewhere about 6' by 3'. I lifted one of these and sort of scraped a hole under the ground. It was very, very loose soil there at the time. As I say, we were getting into April and I was able to scrape a big enough hole. I took a couple of blankets down with me and wrapped them around myself and replaced this part of the flooring. I can't recollect how long I stayed down there now; I know I stayed there over a day. I had to make sure that the whole camp was clear and, lo and behold, when I did come up all of the troops had gone on their march and there was I left in the camp with nobody else there. The gates were open and it was just like a ghost camp.

I knew that the hospital was a quarter of a mile down the road, so I proceeded to make my way to the hospital, and my thoughts were correct in as much as they had left all the injured and sick in the camps to be looked after by one or two male nurses, British male nurses, and there were one or two stragglers that were able to get to the hospital as well, including myself and this became the haven of rest until such times as the American forces arrived. I suppose that the date would be somewhere around about 19 April 1945.

The main objective now was to try and find some food as we were all fairly hungry and had to get some kind of sustenance. I think a couple of New Zealanders and Australians went out and they found a sack of sugar, a couple of live sheep and some potatoes, and in they came into the camp and immediately set about setting up some cooked food. Within an hour these sheep were on the spits being cooked and everybody was looking forward to a glorious meal. Well, I suppose one has got to try and recollect now that our stomachs were pretty weak. Over the years we had had nothing solid in our stomachs and I suppose our stomach muscles weren't operating correctly. Meat in this form we had never seen and the prospects of eating this food was overcome by the fact that we were very, very hungry. So I know I set about eating the meat that I suppose wasn't one hundred per cent cooked and the potatoes. I developed a very serious illness at that time, of colic and food poisoning and I was very, very sick and I could hold nothing down. I was fairly skinny at the time and all I could do was to lie on my bed and just hope that this would depart. I know I used to burn things, burn potatoes black to try and eat the charcoal because someone said if you eat the charcoal it will stop the dysentery and give you some relief.

Things did improve a little but I can always remember on Sunday the 22nd April at 4 o'clock someone rushed into the hospital and said, 'The Americans have arrived, they're here!' My only remark was, 'About bloody time too!' We had been waiting for them to come I suppose for about two or three days. It was an American on a motorbike. A little while afterwards the main force arrived and set up camp around the perimeter of the hospital where they stayed for two or three days.

I would like to harp back if I could to one amusing incident that I forgot to mention about the camp and that was the exercise of going out collecting wood for the purpose of the escape committee or for ourselves to keep warm. In this particular instance, if you remember, everywhere was snow and we did have a small axe that we were given for the purpose of cleaning up the trees so that they could be set up in such a way that we could carry them, and also a knapsack on our backs for us to put twigs in for extra firewood. On one particular day that we went out on one of these forages for wood I was with one of my colleagues and we noticed some animal footprints running through the trees and obviously they were young deer because Germany was well-noted for its deer in the forests. It must be remembered at the time that Goering was in charge of all forests; I forget the title that he was given at the time and nobody was allowed to shoot an animal, least of all any deer that were running around. It was a capital offence from what I was given to understand but in this particular case I noticed that the tracks were running along the edge of the woodland, and in my optimism I said to my colleague that I reckoned if we set up a noose there, there would be a feasible chance that one of the young deer would walk straight into it. We had some rope with us and we set up, or at least, I set up this noose, judged the height at which I thought it was possible to walk through and hopefully the next time we came down we would possibly catch a deer. I mean this was as far as I was concerned, a million to one shot but we had nothing to lose by trying it, and around about a fortnight afterwards we had to go to the same place for collection of trees and timber and, lo and behold, there was a young deer which had strung itself up, having walked straight through this noose.

Now I know this sounds a fantastic story as though one could say, 'Well that's a load of bull', but you have just gotta believe me that there was the deer frozen, strung up on the noose. Well, the biggest problem now was to get some of the meat back to camp, so with the axe we cut off one of the two of the hindquarters of the meat and placed it in our haversacks with twigs over the top of it, and the rest we buried in the snow as deep as we could to ensure that it was there when we came back to get a bit more meat. We duly arrived back in the camp unaware that our backsides were absolutely covered in blood because as the meat thawed out on our bodies then it released the blood which completely saturated our backsides.

How the Germans never tumbled it I'll never know because when you arrive into a camp you arrive in a very small compound where they sort of check you over to see that you haven't stolen anything or bought anything back into the camp that you shouldn't have. They were pretty nonchalant these days I suppose. There we were, pretty worn out with all our timber and trees and, of course, we arrived back into the camp and everybody in the hut had a good feed of venison. Not an awful lot but enough for a couple of meals, it lasted us a couple of days. The irony of it all was that when we went back to collect some more venison the wolves had beaten us to it. The wolves had arrived and, of course, they had smelt the track underneath, and they had got the carcass out and by the time we arrived all that was left were the bones. That was the episode of catching the deer. I'm always reluctant to tell people this story because, as I say, it does seem far-fetched but that was a true story.

However, to go back to the time when the Americans arrived. As I said, they set up camp on the perimeter and they were there for a few days and I began to recover sufficiently enough to walk around. I got attached to one of these Americans who was going into Nuremberg to pick up some supplies, I'm not sure at this moment, and he gave me a ride into Nuremberg and the civilian public there accepted what was happening; there was no ill feeling of any sort, just sort of stared and glared at you but no verbal abuse or anything like that. I think that everybody was in such a state of shock at this stage at the way the German army had completely collapsed, and there were very few soldiers to be seen. Any that were seen were obviously captured and put into compounds. I had the fortunate experience of being able to go into the Nuremberg sports plaza there and anybody who lived through the War would remember the rantings of Hitler when he used to give his rally speeches. He used to fill up the Nuremberg sports ground where he got up on his big podium and he would spend an hour or so in his wonderful speeches that he used to give to the German population and to the troops. I had the privilege, I call it a privilege I suppose, of being able to go up on this podium and stand where Hitler stood, and I remember the American saying to me, 'There you are, that is something you will be able to tell your children when you get back home.' I suppose every time

I see it now in the historical films of the War I remember that I was on Hitler's podium in Nuremberg I will always recollect that, at one stage, I stood where he gave his moral-building speeches.

It was after a couple of days there that we were then taken to the Nuremberg airport to be transported to England. I didn't know what had happened to the main force that had left Stalag 383. They were still under the control of the Germans because they were being pushed further into Germany with the Germans but as far as I was concerned I was virtually free. I don't suppose one could call it really an escape. It was the fact that I was able to get away from the main force and get back to England two or three weeks earlier than it was able to. We arrived at the Nuremberg airport, were given numbers and were to be taken back on American Dakotas. I think they carried around about twenty-five passengers. I was very fortunate to be allocated to a plane that was going to take us straight back to Swindon. At that time, still very sick, I went through to the hospital and saw a Yugoslav doctor. He examined me and he said, 'Look, I think you should be hospitalised. I don't think you are in a fit state to be taken home. You have severe blood poisoning and you have colic.'

I said, 'Well, this ticket I have got in my hand I have been waiting four years for and I am very sorry but I am taking that plane.'

'Well,' he said, 'it is over to you but I would advise that you go into hospital.' But anyway I ignored him and I decided to take the plane back to, as I thought England, and some time in the afternoon we all gathered together, at least the twenty-five of us that were going on this particular plane. We all crouched ourselves into the Dakota and it went to take off at the runway. As it went through the runway ready to take off both the tyres were blown by shrapnel that was lying across the flight path. I can still see the grin on the pilot's face, because these planes are completely open, and the pilot and copilot are not blanketed off at all from us, just more or less sitting with us. This big yankee grin turned around and said, 'Gee boys, you were lucky there.' And, of course, the plane was able to stop and we all disembarked. It took another couple of hours before the next plane was available for us and, fortunately again, this one was going to England because most of them were going to Brussels in Belgium. This time we got off into the air and as he approached the Channel he descended and said, 'I will take you over the white cliffs of Dover,' and he hedge-hopped his way over the English countryside – a very nostalgic feeling, I can tell you, after being away from England for nearly six years, well five years anyway counting the desert. As he went across England, he had to gain height to make his landing. I don't know what went wrong with my stomach. I hadn't eaten for days but, all of a sudden, I became airsick and I was terribly sick while the plane was in the process of landing, and what must have happened was I must have released all the poisons in my body, but I didn't know this at the time.

We duly arrived on the ground and were taken to the big hangars where we were given a shower, our clothes were disinfected and we had a rough check over that we were carrying no visible signs of disease or anything like that. I did feel a lot better after being airsick and we were taken into a big hangar, with hundreds of prisoners sitting down at tables, and on the table was a beautiful roast dinner with a bottle of English beer put in front of us. All of this was done by the WAAFs and we were duly made quite a fuss of. I am not sure how long I stood or sat watching this dinner and watching everybody else eat because for days now I had been dead scared of putting anything into my mouth and trying to consume it, but after quite a space of time, twenty minutes or so, I thought, 'To blazes with it, here goes', and I tucked into that dinner and the bottle of beer and, lo and behold, I held everything. I attribute it to the airsickness that I had had. It must have released all the poisons in my stomach and I was able to proceed and eat what I wanted.

Once I started to eat I consumed everything I saw that was edible. I put on three and a half pounds a day until I reached thirteen and a half stone. All advice given by doctors over the radio to mothers and wives to be careful with what they gave the returned soldiers to eat seemed to fall on deaf ears, and I had no ill effects whatsoever.

When I arrived back in England I rang my parents but was unable to give them any specific day that I might arrive home. They waited there for me to arrive and I know my father had to walk down to the bus stop, which was about 300 yards from our home. Right alongside of it was a public house called the Harrow, which was the local pub and the bus that came along was the number 87. I suppose one came along every ten or fifteen minutes, but my father spent three days waiting at that bus stop for me to arrive, and I think that every time a bus went by he went into the pub for a drink. I think he was inebriated for those four days that he was waiting for me. I did duly arrive, quite an emotional time because I had to walk up a hill and there were houses on both sides of the street. It was a fairly main busy street and, of course, then everybody got to know I had arrived. It was quite an emotional feeling coming through the street and coming home and meeting the family after all those years.

One of the biggest problems I had was that, having arrived home two to three weeks earlier than the main force and as you may recall in the earlier part of the book, most of the company that I was in were local content, they were local people. Most of the people worked at my workplace at the Beckton Gas Works and, of course, everybody knew one another and my biggest problem was that they knew that I'd arrived. Their sweethearts or their mothers or their wives were coming round and asking me if I had seen so and so and when would they be coming home and I'd just cross my fingers and say, 'Don't worry; they will be home anytime. I can't tell you exactly when because I broke away from them but you can rest assured that they will come home', and oh I hoped they would do. Fortunately enough, they all did arrive home but they were three weeks later than myself. I was very pleased about that.

The emotional scene when you arrive home with your family is something that is very, very difficult to explain in a book. When you think of the trials and tribulations that wives, sweethearts and mothers go through when they are first of all told that you are 'missing believed killed'. Then they have to wait four or five months before they get some confirmation in the form of a letter from you to say that you are in a prisoner of war camp, and then they go through the trials and tribulations of receiving letters from you in different parts of Germany and hoping that someday, somewhere we are all going to be back together again. One of the things I didn't mention in the past about the content of the prisoner of war camp was I think one of the biggest tragedies that you had to succumb to was the watching of various friends of yours who had letters from home where their wives had decided to depart or their sweethearts decided to leave them for better fields, and the fact that possibly they may never come back again and when you are in a situation in a prisoner of war camp like this there is nothing you can do about it. Letters don't seem to solve the problem and the anguish and the worry that some people went through because of these situations was really a traumatic experience for them to have to go through. It was one of the real tragedies of the War and I know that dozens and dozens of the prisoners had the same experience that, when they came home, they came home to nothing; their wives or sweethearts had left them. One or two got letters to say that they didn't want any more to do with a person who was prepared to give themselves up and not fight for their country, little knowing that what we had to go through in fighting a war in Europe against Germany at that time.

We arrived back in civil life and we weren't in what you'd call a fit state for meeting the civilian life according to the experts. After a few days at home we were sent to what they call a rehabilitation centre, and in this case I had to go to Great Missenden where I spent three months adapting myself to civil life. Everybody thought they were a bit light-headed. Obviously, our personalities had completely changed. The fear that we had been living with, for the past four years, not being able to speak to civilian people let alone talk to women was something that it took a long time to get used to, and I think, probably one of the great things that happened to me and our compatriots was that we were put into these particular camps to get readjusted to life. We had no, what you would call, army training. We had army training as such that we had the discipline but the ranks that we held meant nothing at the time until we came out of the camp, and with interviews, medical examinations, discussions, talks, and so on and so forth, gradually we came back to what we'd call the sanity of life and we were able to meet all the modern-day events that were happening. After I had spent three months at Great Missenden I went for an interview for an assignment which was to take up the period prior to my demobilisation. After some discussion with the Colonel he said he was transferring me to a German POW camp somewhere in the North of England. I looked at him in complete shock and suggested that this was not a good idea. He said, 'Why not?'

I answered, 'After four years under the Germans as a prisoner of war, being humiliated, starved and ill-treated, do you really expect me to conform to your standard. I'm sorry but I could not.'

He then agreed that it wouldn't be a good idea and, as an alternative, I was given an assignment in an Italian POW camp in the north of Wales. I spent a pleasant time there as there was not much work other than supplying rations for the whole camp on a daily basis.

Here I spent many happy evenings playing the piano in various pubs for the troops. Some public houses used to compete for my playing as the lads used to check where I was going so they could also go there for the evening. On many occasions I was offered cash and all the beer I could drink. I refused these offers saying that I came for my own pleasure and would prefer to come when I felt like it. They all got a turn. I thought this was fair. It was at this camp that I completed my time in the Army and was demobbed in the middle of September 1945.

I suppose in one particular case I had a complete personality change. I walked into the Army a very meek person on the basis that, well, you must do this and you can't do that, and so on and so forth, and you kept your life in a straight line and never deviated from it. But coming out of the Army, and going through all the trials and tribulations you went through, you decided that there was a world waiting out there for you and it was all yours it you decided to make an attempt to take it.

So I became an entirely different person. I suppose most other people did as well but I'm just talking about myself at this particular stage. So I became more strong-willed, more determined, my outlook on life was entirely different. Instead of the meek young chap that walked into the Army in 1939, and after the three months I suppose it took me to settle down, I had no fear of anything. I went out and enjoyed myself, probably drank a little more than I should have done but this is all what I put down to a process of readjustment because it levelled out in the end. I had a particular friend that I was very closely attached to and we did go out enjoying ourselves, and that is all we thought about at the time. We didn't think about work. We didn't have a lot of money. I think we started off our prisoner of war life accumulating 1/6 a day and this gradually went up over the period of the war to 8/6 so I probably came away when I was demobbed with about £450 – I suppose quite a reasonable amount of money in those days but nevertheless it didn't last too long, so one had to get back to work after a period of time and start earning a living.

After two or three months I decided to go back to work and I went back to Beckton Gasworks and got myself established there. I got a permanent situation and did very well and gained promotion through the ranks of what you call gas works from horizontal retorts on to vertical retorts and became foreman of the area, and as a young man I thought I was doing quite well; as a matter of fact I was one of the youngest foremen there at the time.

This is a cover of a book that was produced by ex-Prisoners of War of Camp 383. All proceeds from this book were donated to the Red Cross for the magnificent work they did for prisoners of war . . .

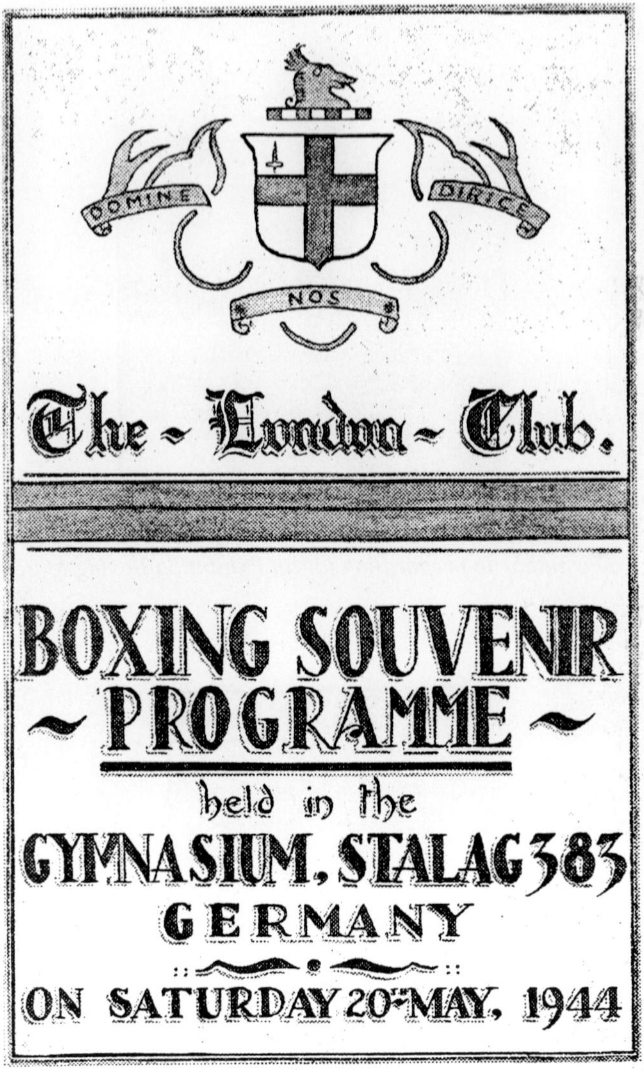

The London Club was formed from within Stalag 383 and from time to time held sporting events. This is an illustration of the front cover of one of their programmes.

The author in preparation for an Exhibition Boxing Match.

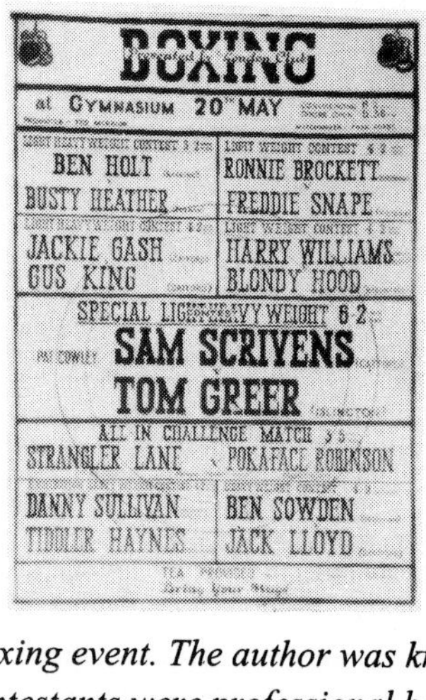

A programme for a boxing event. The author was known then as Ben Holt. Several of these contestants were professional boxers in civilian life.

Photographs of POWs in labour camp in West End Strausse in Munich during 1941 winter. The author is in the lower picture marked with an X.

Photograph of three great friends taken just prior to going overseas in 1940. Top – Author. Left – Cpl. Stevens. Right – Cpl. Saunders.

The crew of the HMS Havock at the beginning of the War

HMS Havock just prior to the outbreak of the War

No 66 Parking Road, Romford where my wife and I lived before leaving to live in New Zealand.

The home in King Edward Road, Barking where my parents moved to when I was four years of age.

CHAPTER FIVE

It was about this time I did meet a very nice young lady. It was purely by chance more than anything else. I was going to a particular farewell evening party to say goodbye to two ladyfriends of mine. These two ladies were emigrating to America. We were going to a particular maisonette in Collier Row just north of Romford in Essex and there had been a blind date arranged for me as I was the only one without a female partner. We went to Romford to pick up this particular girl, but she didn't turn up, so we went and had a beer at the local pub in the High Street in Romford and decided, as there was a dance up at the local hall, we would go up there to see if we could find a young lady who would accompany me to this party. On arrival at the dance hall, I looked around and I saw a very nice young lady standing all on her own. I went up and asked her for the dance and, yes, we danced around the floor to a very nice foxtrot, and I said to her, 'Look we are going to an evening party – a couple are going to America – would you like to come with me?' She looked at me in horror as if to say, 'Not on your life! What do you think I am – just a pick-up?' She was actually waiting for her cousin to finish her dance and then they were going home quite disenchanted with the evening. Anyway, I said, 'Before you make a decision come over and meet my friends', and of course with them were the two ladies who were emigrating to America, who made up this party. After a bit of cajoling and talking with them reassuring her that there was no hanky-panky going on, we were able to convince her to come along and the six of us went off to the party. It was a great evening actually; we enjoyed ourselves immensely. We had a few drinks and a nice long chat and I got to learn quite a bit about her and I think it was about 3 o'clock in the morning when I finally took her home to Romford where she lived. Of course her cousin, who had lost sight of her at that stage, or she told her that she was going out that evening and would make her own way home, was sitting up waiting for her all night thinking that she had got her throat cut or something like that. But, anyway, we had a wonderful evening and I arranged to meet her the next day and I think I just about met her every day that was available. We seemed to have a lot in common. I suppose we were both at loose ends and we were looking for partners. Her name was Joan.

Soon after I met her I was invited to the home of her brother George and his wife for Sunday tea. I arrived there not knowing what was in store for me. George was a foreman on a housing estate at Harold Hill in Essex assisting in erecting prefab houses for the homeless, and some of the workers were German POWs. The government was telling the public it would be a good gesture to invite some of the POWs into their homes. I sat down to my tea with a German POW opposite me. This was soon after my return from Germany where I was a POW and I'm afraid my memory was still vivid with the treatment I had received under the Germans and had my tea feeling quite sick watching this German enjoying British hospitality. When the meal was over I called my lady friend outside and said very firmly, 'Don't ever do that to me again.'

I then told her why. However, this did not spoil a beautiful romance and we both quickly forgot the incident.

A very good relationship developed, and I think within three months we got engaged to be married. We didn't know when we were going to get married because it could take eighteen months to two years to accumulate sufficient money. We were both working. I took her round to meet my parents. At about this time the people who had taken over the maisonette, and were friends of ours, had been told they were being transferred to Rhodesia. He was working for the Ford Motor Company at the time. This transfer meant that they had to sell their furniture when vacating the maisonette. The landlord said he would find a tenant to take over the property and furniture.

As this did not eventuate he said, 'Well look, I haven't been able to find anybody. If you can find someone, so well so good.'

So I got a telephone call one evening to say, 'Look, Fred, when do you intend getting married?'

I said, 'Good gracious me, I think it will be some time yet.' I said we had got to accumulate these finances and everything and make all the preparations and it would take some time. We were looking at somewhere around two years.

'Oh,' he said, 'Only my flat has become available and you could have it if you want it, if you are in a position to buy the furniture.'

'Well,' I said, 'I can't give you a decision right now. Obviously, I have got to talk to my fiancée.' She happened to be in the house at the time that this discussion was going on in another room. So immediately I put the phone down I said, 'Would you like to come for a walk?' So we went for a walk and I explained to her the surprise that I had for her and what was available.

Well, I was thirty years of age and she was twenty-seven, so we were a pretty mature couple and we seemed to know what we wanted. Within two or three days I had rung back and said that we would take it. I think the furniture cost us about £350. It was only a maisonette, one and a half bedrooms, lounge and small kitchen with a front and back garden, very newish-type place and it was the ideal way in which to start a home. I can always remember that having decided on this I took her around to the maisonette and we looked it over, the furniture and everything, and she sat one end of the room and I sat the other. I said, 'Well, we had better go and get married pretty quick, otherwise the neighbours are going to start talking', and that was it. We got a special licence. I went home to my mother and father and said, 'What are you doing on Thursday, Pop?'

He said, 'I don't think I'm doing anything, son. What's the problem?'

I said, 'We are going to get married by special licence.' So on this particular Thursday we went to the Romford registry office with my mother and father, and her brother. We got married and we went down to the Bell and Gate, which was the local pub on the corner. They came to the house and we had a drink and, of course, I had to go to work the next day; couldn't get any leave or anything like that. We had no such thing as a real honeymoon and we carried on our life. Needless to say, all the neighbours and everybody in the street were watching my young wife very inquisitively to see if this was a shotgun wedding, which it wasn't, and we proceeded to enjoy life.

We went on to have thirty-nine years of very happy, married life. From there, life of course proceeded on and I decided I wasn't satisfied in the job I was doing and the application came up for a training course for an outside representation of the Gas Board. It was a nine-month course which I took at Fulham and went to night school four nights a week and got my Gas by Consumer Service Certificate and passed my training at Fulham and was allocated an outside job in a big showroom in a development area in Romford. This was a great move that I made because I didn't have to do shift work. I worked locally and I established myself quite well in this area. We were developing there what we called satellite towns in England at that time removing people from the densely populated London areas, East London areas, into the satellite areas. In this particular case, this area was called Harold Hill, just north of Romford, and it finished up with a population of about 45,000. I was in charge of the area with installation of all gas equipment such as cookers, heaters, water-heaters, washing-machines, you name it. It was a very demanding job – very competitive because you were competing against electricity.

At this time I always had a yearning for wanting to either go to Australia or New Zealand, and I suppose once every month my wife and I used to go up to New Zealand House and look around these places and see what was available. One of the unfortunate things, of course, was the occupation that I had did not qualify me for what you'd call a limited cost fair. I tried various methods of being able to do this but, as I say, the qualifications that I had, which were good, didn't come under the category of the types of occupation that Australia and New Zealand wanted at that time. I spent an awful lot of time with the people in the prisoner of war camps and got to like them very much. I felt that this was where my future lay and when I proposed to my wife and we got engaged I said that if ever I wanted to emigrate to Australia or New Zealand would she have any objections to coming, and she said no. Of course, in her particular case her mother and her father had just recently died and she didn't have her parents to console with a problem like this. I did and I will tell a little more about this later.

I was now forty-two years of age, and had established myself quite well in a job. We had our own home which we were buying; we had a car and, at this stage, we were both working. No children were on the horizon – it was unfortunate that we weren't able to have any children at that stage for whatever reasons, we'll never know. We did console ourselves by becoming 'Uncle' and 'Aunty' to two little children from Barnardo's. They used to come to our home every weekend and we became very close to them.

As I have said I was forty-two years of age and I still had a hankering to emigrate to New Zealand. I said to my wife, 'Look, this has got to stop, this yearning for New Zealand.' We had settled for New Zealand at this stage. I said, 'We're either going to go and do something about it this month or we will forget about the whole thing', because at forty-two you have got to start thinking about whether you can readjust yourself in another country.

So around September 27th, we went up to the Shae Savill Line and started talking to them about costs of fares and whether there was a place available on any ship. It transpired there was a booking available on the *Rangitoto* going to New Zealand around about June the following year. We booked our trip there and then and when we got home we set about selling our house, furniture and everything else.

My wife exclaimed, 'Well you didn't waste any time today.'

I said, 'Well I told you we either do something about it or shut up and forget it,' and I said to myself, 'Well this is it!'

It now became a problem of how to tell these two lovely little girls that we were goint to leave England. We discussed this with the matron of Barnardo's as to how we could best break the news, and she suggested that she would start talking to them about New Zealand. On our next visit everything went well and the two girls accepted the fact that we were going.

We put the machinery in progress; we put the house up for sale which we sold very quickly. We had the furniture, all very good furniture, in the home. We virtually had all that sold and I then rang up the New Zealand shipping company and said, 'Look, we have been able to execute all our business here very, very quickly. Is there an earlier boat that we could travel on?'

So he said, 'Well, I have got nothing at the moment but I will ring you. I will put you on first options.'

Within a couple of days he rang me up and he said, 'Look, I do have another vacancy on the *Ruahine* which was part-cargo and part-passenger ship. It carried about 350 passengers. This was the ship that a few years back that Anthony Eden went to New Zealand in. This was part of the suite that he had. He said, 'I advise you to take it as it is a beautiful suite. It will cost you a fraction more, about £20, but I advise you to take it because you will really enjoy the trip.'

So we took the particular accommodation that they set out for us and I paid the rest of the money. Then, at this stage, I had to tell my parents what I was going to do. We both went a round to my parents' home to tell them that we were going to emigrate to New Zealand. I know my mother was sitting there and she said, 'You are always wanting to do something or go somewhere.'

I said, 'Look, I have been nowhere yet and I said this is something that I have always wanted to do. I will never satisfy myself until I have been.'

Of course my father chipped in and said, 'Look, all the years that you've spent establishing yourself in the job that you've got, you've got your own home and your own car. You can't wish for anything better. You are throwing away a lifetime of experience.'

I said, 'Well, this is the challenge that I know in my own heart and soul that I have got to do to find out whether I am right or wrong and I will never be satisfied unless I do it.'

Well, we duly went away that evening with my family very, very upset and I suppose in hindsight, when I think back, I can understand why. I knew I was obsessed with the idea of emigrating and I suppose I didn't think about the implications and the worries that they would have even though I was forty-two years of age. You have got to bear in mind that they waited six years for me while I was away so it was quite an upset for them.

I said to my wife that we must carry on going round there every week; we musn't stop going because quite a lot of animosity had been built up at this time and we went round every Thursday night and nothing was ever said. Nothing was ever mentioned. I tried to get in some sort of discussion about New Zealand to show them where we were going and what we were going to do, but they just weren't interested; it was a closed book. Nobody else spoke about New Zealand for the three months.

We left home and then went to Brentwood to stay with some friends while we were waiting to get on the boat. Regretfully, I have to say that when we did depart at the East India Dock on the *Ruahine* my parents didn't come to see us off and I think one of the unfortunate things was that everybody blamed my wife for taking me to New Zealand which was farthest from the truth. It was I who did all the instigating and she was quite happy to come along with me.

We spent five weeks on the high seas and we had a wonderful time. The ship was not overloaded with passengers. It was one great big holiday and as it happened we met very, very little bad weather. We went through to Perth, Australia and round Australia to Melbourne and Sydney. We did stop at other places, of course. Coming through the Suez Canal I was able to show my wife all the areas that I was in the desert, only by indicating as we went through the canal. Cairo, we stayed there for a couple of days and, as I say, it was quite an eventful trip; we thoroughly enjoyed it. We made our own entertainment, we had our music and we arranged our own dances. The food was excellent and it was one big relaxing holiday, and I suppose only having about 350 passengers on the ship you became very close to one another and you made a lot of friends.

I know in this particular case here that everybody had a lack of exercise and, being a physical training instructor in the Army, I offered through the purser that if anybody was interested in doing physical exercises, if they came up on such and such a deck at 7.30 each morning we would go through some process of keeping ourselves fit. I didn't realise how popular this would be because people from the age of sixteen to sixty had arrived up there for physical training exercises. You can actually make these people completely muscle-bound and do them some injuries, so I had to be very, very careful with the types of people that I had. It was all right with the young people but with the elderly you had to be very careful. Fortunately enough, I got away with it and I split them into two or three different classes so that they all had exercises and training to do that related to their various ages. I did very, very well at this and it remained right through until the end of the trip and, of course, with myself I was getting what you might call superbly fit. There were competitions on the ship like table tennis, deck quoits and all other types of entertainment, for which prizes were given. I know I entered the deck quoits singles, mixed doubles, men's singles and I went through and, being so fit through all this training, reached the finals and won all these three events. Not bad because we had some quite good young turks on the boat that we had to beat.

However, it was a tremendously good trip. I enjoyed every bit of it. Our cabin was first-class; it was right up on top of the deck and we had views of the ocean from our cabin. The trip was one of the best that I have ever had and, of course, quite an experience for my wife as it was her first trip away from England and particularly to the other side of the world. We visited some lovely countries on the way; through the Suez Canal, Cairo and all around Australia, two or three days in Perth and a stopover in Melbourne and a short stay in Sydney.

CHAPTER SIX

We duly arrived in Wellington on a very cool morning. I can remember that winter was approaching and it was beginning to get quite cool from a New Zealand point of view. It was around about April when we arrived so you can imagine the beginning of the New Zealand winter. However, we had nobody to meet us at Wellington. We did have a friend, and he was going to meet us at Napier but we had to have the experience of travelling then from Wellington up to Palmerston North where we had to wait most of the day to get the train to Napier. This was quite an occasion because in quite a lot of the towns in New Zealand in those days trains used to run through the main street of the town, and in Palmerston North this was an occasion where the train actually came right up into the middle of the town.

We duly arrived at Napier and our friend met us, and he did have some accommodation for us in Taradale. The weather was quite cool and we couldn't make much assessment of New Zealand at this stage because we hadn't had a chance to get around. Feeling quite lonely and alone away from all our relatives and friends, this was a vast experience. Of course when we arrived in New Zealand there was no television and very little sealed roads. The main roads were sealed but all bypass roads were metal roads and apart from that it was a very, very, quiet slow-moving country – quite different when coming from the metropolis of London.

However, we were introduced to our friend with whom we were going to stay; she was a widowed woman but a Lancashire woman. She had a very nice home in Taradale and had a son that lived with her. This son would be about 33-34 at the time, and gradually we got introduced to one or two people. We were able to catch up with one friend who was in a prisoner of war camp with me in Stalag 383; only for the last few days. He was captured in Italy. He turned out to be a great friend over the period that I was in Taradale and we settled down.

We decided then that we wouldn't invest any money in a car for a couple of years or so until we got ourselves established but we soon realised that there was very little transportation in New Zealand at that time. There was an intermediate bus service but very scarce, and to be able to get round looking for jobs and things like that, we soon realised after a couple of days we just had to get a vehicle so that we could make ourselves mobile. At this stage we were wearing out shoes like nobody's business because of the lack of footpaths and the sort of rough conditions which we had to walk in. So we bought ourselves a Vauxhall car and in those days every car seemed to be of British origin and Vauxhall seemed to be the predominant car that was running around New Zealand. Anyway, we got this Vauxhall Velox, a reasonably good car. I forget what I paid for it now, much more that I wanted to I know but we realised it was essential if we were going to get around and get into places like Napier to try and get a job.

Now to try and give you some idea of the conditions in New Zealand at that time, and I am talking around about 1957/8, there was no unemployment. The labour exchange was the loneliest place going but at the same time there were very, very little vacancies in work and I can remember that Walter Nash was the prime minister of the day and Nordmeyer was the finance minister. I can very well remember Nordmeyer because he brought in what was termed in those days the Black Budget. Beer, cigarettes and taxes and things like that went up in price quite dramatically. One must remember that in those days the average wage at around about that time was about £12 to £13 a week and people were able to survive on this. Food was relatively cheap; we found that the cost of living was much cheaper here in New Zealand then as opposed to England. Life was much, much slower and we very quickly adapted ourselves.

It didn't take over long for us to find some form of occupation although nothing in the category that I was looking for. My wife was able to get a job in broadcasting. She was a very good shorthand typist. With myself it was quite a different matter. I was going into a new country with pretty good qualifications with regard to references, and so on and so forth, and I found that these were working against me. In other words people were looking at the references and the qualifications that I had and they were afraid that they would probably have to pay me too much money. Little did they realise that I would take any sort of job at that time to work my way through.

I finally got a job, believe it or not, in a wool-carding factory, where they take the wool and clean it, tease it and put it on massive big spools for manufacturing. This was really a terrible job, because we had to work shift work to start with, and working on these carding machines your hands really got cut to pieces. However, it was a job and it was an income, and the most important thing was to start living without sort of drawing on whatever resources that we were able to bring with us. I suppose I stuck this job for about 7, 8 or 9 weeks and in the meantime I was keeping my eyes open for a better sort of occupation. This did come about, a travelling salesman for a paint company – the New Zealand Paint and Varnish Company just outside Taradale, a place called Awatoto.

I very quickly established myself in this job and it meant travelling around the North Island which was good from my point of view because it helped me come to an understanding of the country, to enjoy some of the scenery, and to get acquainted with some of the various types of townships that I was working in. As I say, I established myself quite well and was able to produce some good results drawing on all the talents and training that I had had in England as a salesman, and one of the things that I always said was that when I was coming to New Zealand I would give myself two years and then I would expect to be working for myself. I could never see the point of travelling 13,000 miles, giving up a respectable type of job and carry on the same situation, so I always expected that somewhere along the line I was going to be my own boss.

The other problem, of course, that we had as a married couple it was very difficult to have children. We never knew the reason why. In those days we were told there were no problems but whether it was the chemistry or whatever we were unable to produce children. So we set about then enquiring about adoption in New Zealand and things were much, much better from that point of view than they were in England. We went to two or three different agencies enquiring and we finally settled on the Salvation Army in Napier, where they looked after mothers who were having children out of wedlock. There were quite a few of these in those days and we got associated with a Major Gotham in the Salvation Army at this home. Surprise, surprise and you must remember that at this stage I would be somewhere around about forty-five and my wife would have been forty-one and we found it quite easy to attain adoption. We had to obtain certain forms to fill in and so on so that they could try and match the child to our particular types of personalities, and it wasn't too long before there was a child available.

We had been in the country then, I suppose, about twelve to thirteen months and we got an invitation to come and look at the prospective child. In this particular case it was a girl no more than, I would think, twenty-four hours old, and the mother, who we never saw, was still in the hospital. We were able to see this young child and she was a very, very beautiful baby. Actually it was one of the rare occasions that I saw a new-born baby that was actually fully formed. You know, no creases, absolutely beautiful and we agreed then that we would like to have this young baby and there was no problem at all, and within a fortnight she was ours. The procedure was, that having agreed to take it, my wife would go to the hospital each day for the next fortnight to handle the baby, feed it, change it and bath it so that she got used to it and the baby got used to her.

Of course, she duly gave her notice in at the place where she was working because the idea was that as soon as we could acquire a child she would become a mother and stay at home. And at that time it was one of the greatest moments of our lives that we had a child and it was a wonderful experience, and it turned out to be a beautiful young girl.

About this time my wife had a sister who lived in South Africa. Now because of the difference in ages, my wife who came from a fairly large family of about eight was the last one in the line of the family, born in the later years of her mother's life. So consequently, she never saw much of this sister that she knew that she had in South Africa although they did correspond with one another from time to time, but she never had actually seen her or remembered seeing her. On this basis there was somewhere around seventeen years difference in their ages. She was that much older. Through the correspondence she had said that she would like to come to New Zealand for a three-month holiday. I thought this was a great experience for her and I encouraged it because I thought to myself, 'Well, this is a great chance for her to become associated with a sister that she had never seen.' So we set about inviting her over to stay with us. This would probably take some time but she duly made the arrangements for the arrival into New Zealand. I tell you this because this was about the time when the baby, Janet, which was her name by the way, would have been about three months old when her sister decided that she would come over for three months.

I went down to Wellington to meet her off the boat and easily recognised her by photographs, and duly brought her all the way up to Napier where she stayed with us for three months. She was quite a charming woman in her late sixties. She was what they call a domestic nurse and in those days in South Africa it appeared to me, anyway watching her, that they didn't have to do any domestic work whatsoever. They didn't have to do washing-up; they didn't have to look after their homes. They always had a coloured person to do that work for them. She always remarked about her wonderful Lizzie who used to do all of her work for her and, surprisingly enough, at her age she was quite incapable of doing anything. Even as a domestic nurse they had nurses under them. When they appeared at the homes to look after the ailing members of the family they didn't have to do any work other than just tend to them and talk to them and read to them, and give instructions to other people to do any work like making beds and washing-up or anything like that. It was a great surprise to me to find that here was a person of her age who was quite incapable of doing anything at all other than look after herself. She had wonderful skin. She was a very good-looking woman for her age and she stayed with us for about three months.

We weren't overly sorry that she was going because it became quite a trial to my wife, who was going through the experience of looking after a young baby and, as you can well imagine, a young baby does keep you up during the night-time and we used to take it in turns to console the child and keep her at peace so that she slept well and fed well. Of course, not only that but we had another very big baby who we were looking after at the same time. However, it was an experience. I was thrilled that she was able to be with her sister and enjoy her company but, as I say, in the end, we were a little bit relieved when it was time for her to go back. Life proceeded on quite well. Janet was christened in the Taradale Anglican church and grew up to be, as a child, a very beautiful young girl, and we were very proud.

So having done this we decided that we would then make an application for a further child preferably in this case a brother. We went and saw Major Gotham again and said that we would like to do this, not immediately but some time in the very near future so that there was not too much of a gap between them. And, of course, things were beginning to dramatically change in my life as well. I know that at this stage we had bought a house in Chester Street in Taradale, which was only about three or four hundred yards from where we were staying. With the monies that we had saved we used as a deposit to purchase this two-bedroomed home on a quarter acre section. It was quite a nice home for that time, of wooden structure and tin roof. We were quite happy that we had finally got a home of our own.

CHAPTER SEVEN

Life seemed to settle down quite well. My job at the New Zealand Paint and Varnish Company was established quite well. At about that time there were some rumbles with regard to the local councils in Taradale, and I had a group of people come along to me to ask if I would stand as a councillor in the area. I said, 'Come off it. I have only been over here eighteen months and you expect me to be able to get the support of the whole town and get elected.'

They said, 'Well, we think that you would probably be the man we need to give a new look to the town.'

I was quite honoured with the fact that they had come along and offered me this opportunity to put myself up as a candidate, but at that particular time I said I would need a lot of time to think about it. I thought that it would be quite a hard battle because of my identity in the town and the fact that I had only been in New Zealand a short space of time. However, two months afterwards they came back again and wanted to know whether I had thought about it and would I consider putting myself forward as a candidate for the Council. So we sat down that evening and we started talking about a policy of how we would do it. I said that I would expect that they would be part of a team that would support me in a form of advertising and meeting the public. So we, in due course, put my name forward as a candidate and at this particular time we had to find seven councillors to form the committee for the local borough. I knew I had a tremendous job on my hands and one or two people of the town had indicated – 'Boy!' they said, 'you are bashing your head up against a brick wall here, you know. You will never break down the business people of the town.'

There was a lot of disenchantment with the progress of the Borough and I think this was the reason why one or two people were looking for some fresh faces to get the whole place a new look. Anyway, having accepted it I set about planning the campaign. All costs of promoting myself had to come from my own pocket, and I formally paid my deposit and we set about a process of getting to know the people. I really worked hard at it. I set about trying to meet everybody in Taradale. Although it was only a small borough of around about 4,500 people (ratepayers), it took a lot of work outside my working hours and at weekends to meet people, to attend certain meetings and to make myself popular with the people as an independent candidate for the Borough of Taradale.

The election day came along and we were in a position then to just have a sit back and keep our fingers crossed and wait, and see exactly how things would go. I had already met the existing mayor who had put his name up again and not very many people gave me very much of a chance of getting sufficient votes to get through. However, that evening we were all sitting round listening to the radio waiting for the figures to come through and around about 9.30 that Saturday evening the figures came through, and, would you believe it, we polled the second highest of the whole fourteen candidates that had put forward. The only person that came in front of me was a woman and this was, to me, a tremendous achievement. Of course the first person to ring me up was the mayor and he said, 'Well, Mr Holt, I didn't think you had a chance. You must have worked tremendously hard and congratulations.'

Well, my popularity increased to the extent that I was put onto the Works Committee and life began to take on a little bit more importance, and for about eighteen months I progressed quite well as a councillor for Taradale. Important issues were coming up at that time like stormwater drainage and sewerage, to which there was a lot of public opposition because of the cost of rates at that time but in hindsight now, although we got this thing pushed through even against some public opinion, it was one of the best things that we did for the local area because the cost structure of putting it in was far less than it would have been today.

Things started to move quite well at that time. It was my intention that I would never remain working for a boss for ever having given up everything to come to a new country. I wanted to establish myself in my own business. Having what I call a reasonably good public profile and at the same time having good public relations in the form of sales techniques and dealing with the public, I felt possibly that this was the sort of line that I should attend to, and one of the propositions that came up was in the form of private hotels. I happened to see an ad in the local paper in Napier of a private hotel leasehold that was up for sale on the Marine Parade of Napier. I went and had a look at this. It was fairly run-down but I could see potential in it because of its location and because of the need of what I call good family hotel accommodation. You must remember that at this time there were no such things as motels in New Zealand. They were mainly what we call licensed hotels and what we call private hotels in the form of bed and breakfast or full board. I had a good look at this and I discussed it with my wife at the time. I knew that there was going to be a tremendous amount of hard work involved and our little girl was just approaching two years of age and it meant another complete transformation. It meant also that I would have to give up my job as Councillor, sell my house and eventually move into the hotel as all part of the business.

Anyway, all the details were completed and we set about taking over the lease of this particular private hotel. The name of it was Capeview Hotel which I retained right throughout the time that I owned it. It was situated on the Marine Parade which was roughly about half a mile from the centre of the town. It looked out over the Pacific and you had quite a good view of the coast line from Napier to Hastings. As I said, it was a tremendous amount of work in negotiating the whole thing for it was fairly run-down. When we took over the business there was very little goodwill attached to it but, nevertheless, I set to over the period of a couple of years establishing it into one of the best private hotels with the best clientele on the Marine Parade. It would be true to say that we had people from all walks of life and most parts of the world. We got ourselves associated with the Government Tourist Bureau, and we finished up buying the lease so that we owned the property. We had two domestic staff working for us and during the holiday periods and seasonal periods we always had the place quite full which was quite an achievement.

I had quite advanced ideas for this place in buying properties around it and probably converting the whole area into a motel situation but this demanded, once again, a tremendous amount of work. We did expand in that we bought the property alongside and turned it into a cafeteria with an outside boulevard, tables and chairs and seating capacity of about thirty-five people. By the way, the capacity of the hotel was about thirty beds which provided us with a fairly good income when the holiday season was in full swing. Being a seasonal type of place we had to make sure that the business was paying for itself during the winter period when things were very, very quiet. This was done by taking on training agencies from the Post Office and the Railway at reduced rates which kept the whole business ticking over while we were waiting for the season, at the same time carrying out, what I call, modernisation repairs to lounges and dining rooms and bedrooms and so on and so forth. And, as I say, we finished up with what I would call a very good hotel and quite profitable. We converted the place next door into a cafeteria and, once again, it turned out to be quite a success because it complemented the hotel in such a way that, although the hotel provided what we call dinner, bed and breakfast, this followed up with providing luncheons and afternoon teas to the people in the hotel. Also it supplied other holiday-makers with a place in which to come and have good lunches, and I say this was very successful to the extent that we had two people employed in this particular situation.

I was working tremendous hours and I know that a couple of times I was under my doctor because of the strain of the work that I was putting in. He told me I had got to ease up but, ignoring this and just telling him to give me something to keep me going, I was able to carry on working at least eighteen hours a day, and I suppose one could call me at that time a workaholic. I still enjoyed what I was doing; I was a very fit man and I felt in my own mind that I could meet the capacity of work that was demanded of me. I suppose I was one of these people that always felt that if you wanted to do a good job you do it yourself even though I had staff working for me that were doing what I would call the normal mundane work of serving and cleaning the place up. All the administrative work I did myself. I tried to keep my wife away from as much of the work as possible. She did help but I tried to ensure that she devoted her time to our little daughter who was turning out to be a lovely young girl, and it was no hindrance to us during the business, and we would make sure that her lifestyle was never affected. She had the benefits of meeting a lot of people and a lot of other children as they came into the hotel, and in a way it was a growing-up benefit for her.

We made a lot of friends, and one or two even after all these years I am still able to meet and enjoy their company. We got to the stage of close to five years of running this business, and I was approached by one of the staff who said to me that if I ever intended to sell the business would I give them the first opportunity of purchasing it. At that time I was not considering it but I did realise that I had devoted a lot of my time selfishly towards this business. I felt my wife had backed me up very, very well and for one reason or another we went back to these people who were looking at the possibility of purchasing it. They used to come in and work for us and, always seeing the place full and how nice it always looked, they looked at this as a good money-spinner, not really realising the amount of work that I was putting into it.

Anyway, discussions went forward and their parents came down as well and we discussed the question of the sale. We came up with a figure and a rent because they would only be buying the lease and that they would take over the business at the beginning of the new financial year which was the 1st April the following year. At about that time, August, we would be soon approaching the beginning of the high season and they came back to me again and said, 'What would be the figure of the sale if you gave it to us before Christmas?'

This would be around about the end of October. Well, bearing in mind that I had so many thousand pounds worth of pre-bookings which I relied upon, I then set about with my solicitor sorting out a new figure. This was once again accepted and so we duly handed over the business around about October still carrying on the cafeteria for a further six months.

About six months prior to this we had another letter from South Africa from my sister-in-law Gwen, who had previously come over for the three months, and she was asking at that time could she come over and live permanently with us in New Zealand. We knew this was quite a problem because of the lifestyle which she enjoyed in South Africa that was totally different to the lifestyle we had here. I think I mentioned before that she had the inability to do anything domestically as she always had somebody to run around and do all these mundane jobs for her. So I, once again thinking of my wife and how wonderful it would be to have her sister over here with whom she had had very, very little contact, wrote her a very long letter explaining to her the lifestyle of New Zealand and how she would have to completely readapt her life and there would be no little coloured person running around doing all the odd jobs for her and that she would have to learn to stand on her own two feet. Now I am asking a woman here of around about the age of sixty-eight or sixty-nine to completely change her life. Anyway, we sent the letter off and in a very short space of time we received a letter back saying that she understood, having been over here previously, what she would have to do and she would still love to come. I'd like to point out that this was before the sale was negotiated for the hotel.

So anyway, everything was completed and we sent off another letter inviting her over bearing in mind the letters I had written to her explaining the big changes that she would have to participate in in her life and on that basis if she understood that she would be quite welcome to come over and join us. She indicated at that time that she had a few bits of furniture that she would have to send over prior to her arriving, and we said this was OK. We were due to go on holiday, for a few days rest and friends of ours were coming over to take over the hotel and look after it while we were away. We were going to Taupo and around Gisborne with our little daughter, and about two days prior to our departing, one of the biggest pantechnicons you have ever seen arrived at the back of the hotel. This was the bits and pieces that my sister-in-law said she was sending over. It was a complete household of furniture, cutlery, you name it; we had the lot of this and this was just prior to going on this holiday of ours and the whole back section of the hotel had been completely loaded up with cases. Well, all this had to be unpacked and put away because we didn't know what the weather was going to be and it all had to be put under cover. I think we worked mainly through the night; a friend came down and helped me. Beautiful furniture, a lot of it was made out of South African stinkwood and I still retain one or two pieces of this now. As I say, all of this furniture had to be packed to mix into the hotel furniture, which we duly completed of course, but it was a tremendous amount of work. I had never seen so much furniture arrive in all my life. This arrived three months before she was due to come over. Anyway, she duly arrived and we set her up in the home that we had bought on the hill realising with all this furniture I would have to invest in another property.

CHAPTER EIGHT

We bought a very nice property on the top of a hill with a half-acre section overlooking the Pacific. It was a Maori Te atu Trust land, the site of the old Hukarere Maori Girls' School, which I understand some years ago got burnt down, so the land was leased out and the property that I lived in was a very old colonial home that had a lot of great features about it. We enjoyed it tremendously. It was virtually two homes in one on top of each other. The top of the building was level with the roadway and the bottom, being on a sort of gradient you walked around so that the bottom of the house also had a front door. The top part of it was let, and we took over and lived in the bottom. It was a delightful spot, wonderful views and delightful grounds. So we deposited our sister-in-law in this place which she would live in while we were still negotiating the sale of the hotel. She lived there on her own looking after herself, whilst we were still back at the hotel. This was a good experience for her because, as I said before, she never had the ability to look after herself. There was always someone running around to do her cooking and clean up for her but it was a good experience for her to get adjusted to the New Zealand way of life.

We carried on at the hotel until such times as the sale went through and they took over in October in the year of 1964. So they were able to start with full bookings right through until at least the end of February, which was the major profit margin for the year and the high season. We carried on with the cafeteria and this was again a seven-day-a-week business, the weekends sometimes being the busiest when most other outlets were closed and, whereas today we enjoy a seven-day shopping period, in those days most outlets closed on a Saturday and a Sunday.

Cafeterias were probably the only places that were open. It was quite a good business. I enjoyed it because it gave me a flair for cooking and I established a very good clientele, and one of these outlets, of course, was taxi-drivers, and the reason for this was the ample parking space. Although it was half a mile from the centre of the town, they were able to come up and relax in their tea times with no worry about parking. So we were able to accommodate all their business and, when they had to have meals and sandwiches and teas taken down to their office in town, we got the orders for it. We produced a wide range of goods from steaks to pies and omelettes. I was well-renowned for my omelettes. Everybody who enjoyed an omelette always came to Capeview to have one. It was quite an interesting form of occupation. The only disadvantage of it was that it was seven days a week and you did have very quiet periods at times.

However, there was a particular taxi-driver at this time who was interested in the business and he thought that he would like the opportunity of purchasing it. This happened in both cases. I never put the businesses up for sale. They were always acquired by somebody who was interested in looking at the ways of owning a business. So with this opportunity very quickly a sale went through for the purchase of the leasehold of the building. This meant that I would still have a reasonably good income from the hotel and the cafeteria which paid for the upkeep and mortgage of my own home that we'd bought up in Hukarere Road.

So at this time we were, as I have mentioned before, very interested in adopting another child to be a brother to Janet, and indications were that this was just about to happen, and so in some respect I was pleased that the sale was going through because I could devote more time to my wife and family. My wife had been very, very good to me while I was in business and I thought this might be a good idea to have a rest from it and to probably go into something else a little later. As the sale did materialise and the new tenants took over the cafeteria, it was almost simultaneously that we had the opportunity of adopting Peter. Once again we had him right from the first week he was born, a lovely little baby and he came from the same source of Major Gotham at the Salvation Army in Napier. We thought that everything was right at that time; everything we'd asked for we had got. So I felt that it was time to go back to the old country in England and show my family what we'd done and what we'd achieved.

By this time, as I told you earlier, the relationship was not very good between my parents and us, but a lot of this had been mended by correspondence and tapes, and everything seemed to get back onto good family relationships once again, which I was very pleased about. So I set about making preparations for a holiday in England and we decided to make this a seven-month tour going by boat both ways and taking the two children with us. This came about quite comfortably and we sailed in 1966.

Peter was just about coming up to one year of age. He was about nine months old when we decided to go to England. We proceeded to book a boat trip to England and a boat trip back – one going through the Panama Canal and the other back through the Suez so we did the whole round trip, visiting several countries on the way. Quite the most enjoyable trip out, it took five weeks. As I say, Peter was then around about one year of age and Janet was coming on six.

It was very, very warm crossing the equator but we were arriving in England at around about the March period. I remember this quite well as I spent my fiftieth birthday back home at the house where I had been brought up since I was eleven years of age in Ripple Road. The unfortunate thing about it was that winter wasn't over in Britain at that time and coming from New Zealand, which had a warmer climate, and travelling through the Tropics and enjoying beautiful weather on our way to England, arriving in March was probably the wrong time of year to arrive in England with a family and we did experience some very, very cold weather. I can distinctly remember April 26th having a snowstorm in Essex where we took our daughter out playing snowballs at the time in the fields at Gidea Park. It didn't last long because it was so cold that we had to get back round the warm fire.

The weather did improve after a time and we had some wonderful times meeting up with all the family and the great enjoyment of showing off my two children, who were at that stage very lovely and made us a complete family. Although he is now twenty-eight I can still remember with great pride my son taking his first steps across the lounge towards my father. Things proceeded well during the holiday and we enjoyed meeting up with all our old friends.

I took my mother and father away for a holiday for a fortnight to Weston-super-Mare which they enjoyed thoroughly, and it made me very happy for us to be altogether like this. I had made my peace with my parents. I felt that I had justified my move to New Zealand and that I had achieved things that they probably didn't expect me to.

As our holiday came to an end something eventful happened. My wife had a brother, George, whose wife had died and he was living on his own. He was working at the Beckton Gas Works at this time but in his early days he had been a seafaring man and had been to Australia and New Zealand. He was a very interesting man to talk to and, like myself, he had had a lot of different experiences in his lifetime. He was a very generous man and had never achieved a lot in his life financially. He was at this stage just supporting himself in his job and living alone, so I spoke to him about coming out to New Zealand and living with us.

Anyway, he said at the time that he didn't think he would have enough money put by to be able to come, so we did our homework and found out what he would get from his works in the form of superannuation, what he could sell his car and other assets for, and we found that he could not only pay his fare but would have £500 over which surprised him. All this did materialise and he gave up his job and he came out with us on the return boat to New Zealand.

At that time we were booked to go back on the *Northern Star* but there was a big shipping strike on in England and it looked at that stage that we would never have the opportunity of getting back to New Zealand at the time we wanted to. Nobody knew at that stage how long the strike would be on. It was a big general shipping strike and it was causing quite a problem at that particular time. So with the Cooks Travel Agency I went through the whole process of trying to get transferred onto another boat and we were able then to get bookings on the *Ellinis* which was the Greek shipping line and regretfully the standards of travelling were nowhere near as good as the Shaw Saville although we did get a refund because of the *Ellinis* travel was much more economical than the *Northern Star*. However, we did tolerate it and it was adequate up to a point but, as I said, the standards were nowhere near as good as the standards we would have had on the *Northern Star*. The unfortunate thing about it was, when it was about to leave the port of Southampton the strike was over and I think that possibly we could have taken our booking on the *Northern Star* anyway but no one was to know that, and it was necessary for me to get back to New Zealand after being away for such a long time, and we took the boat trip back through the Suez Canal back around to Perth. We had two or three days stopover there – a most delightful city. One of the cleanest cities I have ever passed through. We spent a day and a half in Melbourne and enjoyed the city; the same with Sydney and then our trip back to New Zealand where we caught up with our sister. Of course George then met her for the first time for many, many years.

CHAPTER NINE

We proceeded to settle down as a reasonably good family. At that time of course, I had no idea of what I was going to do, but I did and was able to get back to a job that I had done previously for a few months and that was in John Anderson's nurseries. While I was in England I did some filming for him at a big nursery in St Albans to show him what went on there so he could possibly learn a bit more about it, although he was world renowned. He used to travel to America and Australia, and Anderson Nurseries at that stage was one of the biggest nurseries in New Zealand. A very progressive man, he took over the business from his father and turned it into a wholesaling exercise. I went back and worked for him for a period of six months while I was waiting to see what I was going to do, and there came an opportunity of opening up a retail shop in a fairly good part of Napier which got to be known as the Balmoral Shopping Centre. It was a shopping mall with seven or eight retail outlets like shoe shops, paint shops, what have you. It occurred to me that, with my experience in painting and wallpapering, I would have a look at opening up a paint and wallpaper shop, first with negotiations with regard to the lease, and I finally decided to take a five year lease and go into competition with all the big boys in paint and wallpaper. I negotiated with one of the biggest paint companies, British Paints, to be my main supplier who were very good to me in initial stock for the shop on a low-cost basis. I set about setting up the shop in the meantime. Of course, I had to give up the occupation that I had, which I classed as only temporary, because Mr Anderson thought that probably money was the problem and he offered me more money but I said, 'No. I am starting up a new business and this is the only reason for leaving.'

So I set about going into business with the paint and wallpaper. It was a very attractive shop but once again paint and wallpaper was a very competitive game and there were a couple of big outlets in Napier that I was competing with, but I always maintained that service was the most important thing and if you could give the service to the public then they would come to you, and I suppose they did in reasonable numbers but it was a struggle. I kept the business for about four years and three months, and it was hard work. Not only did I sell paint and wallpaper but mirrors, paintings and all garden furniture and kitset furniture. To help supplement the income I used to assemble these kitsets for the customers, and I used to varnish and paint them. I used to do all the garden furniture and assemble those and deliver them, and, as I said before, shopping was only a five-day week and no shops were allowed to open except those like corner grocery dairies that were allowed to open on the Saturday and no shops were allowed to open on a Sunday. It did allow me to go down to the shop on several occasions and pick up some of the back work in assembling and painting.

I can remember on one occasion I had the front door of the shop open and I was getting ready to deliver. I had George with me and we were going to load up some garden furniture to deliver, which I was allowed to do because the shop wasn't open, but somebody did come into the shop and they wanted to buy an inch paint brush, and I sold them an inch paint brush. Now whether this was a set up or not I don't know. I don't think that that customer was set up but most unfortunately one of the persons watching shops like mine was a local inspector for shop trading hours, saw this customer come away with the paint brush and immediately came into the shop and reported me for retailing business on a Saturday. The only thing I could ever say to this man was, 'Do you enjoy your job, because I wouldn't have it for all the money in the world.' I mean the shop was not doing a big business. I could have virtually given the man the brush. But I sold it to him because that was his need not my want. Anyway, I got taken to court and I was fined £25. That's what I got for selling a 34p paint brush. However, I couldn't argue against it and that was what happened.

As I said before, the business was a struggle. I found out I had to give up a lot. I didn't lose money over it but then again I didn't make a lot of money and I was able to sell the business, under a certain amount of pressure from the owners of the shopping block, eventually to a retired couple. We had a very close group of friends and we all entertained one another; and we would always be rushing up to Taupo for a weekend fishing, which we enjoyed immensely, on Lake Taupo.

In the meantime I think my sister-in-law became disenchanted with our way of life and there was always a certain amount of friction because she didn't adapt herself fully to the ordinary person's way of life. A little animosity crept in and she finally decided to pack up, and went all the way back to South Africa. I think it was about two or three years after that that we heard she had died. She was in her seventies at that time. I don't know what she died of because it was one of the tragedies that no more communication took part. However, it was an exercise we tried, and everything was done with the best of intentions, but it didn't work out. As I say, if she had become a little more independent in looking after herself and adjusting to the way of life I think that life could have been a little happier, but as it turned out it didn't and she went back.

George, in the meantime, got very good jobs and was a very well-liked man. He was very generous round the home. He was very handy, very adaptable and we got on well with him, but of course here was a case where the father was in New Zealand in the latter years of his life and his two daughters were back in England. He had hoped that his eldest daughter and son-in-law would eventually follow him out to New Zealand. We did our best to try to persuade them but, although his daughter would have loved to have come, his son-in-law was a very English-orientated farm worker and he still enjoyed his job, which he'd had as a very young man working for a very prominent Essex farmer. He is now around about the age of fifty or fifty-five and this is where he will stay until he retires. George used to save his money and give it to me to put away for him, and every New Zealand winter he would go back to England for three or four months with his daughter and then come back out to New Zealand. Obviously, it was not a happy situation because he enjoyed being with his family although he and my wife and myself, we all got on very well together. He came with us wherever we went. He was ten years older than myself and so at around the age of seventy-five I think he went home to England to see his daughter and decided that he would stay there. I think the daughter was pleased because he stayed with her and enjoyed the rest of his life there. On two occasions when I went back to England I used to stay there and met up with George on each occasion.

Perhaps I am jumping the gun here a little because I would like to refer back to a couple of the tragedies that happened in my life. Just before I left the paint shop one morning at around about 11 o'clock, I forget which day it was, I had a call from England from one of my family to tell me that my father had just been run over and killed by a very fast-moving car. My father never drove all his life. The only thing he ever drove was a push-bike and he had never handled a car. A very fit man, he was in his late seventies, seventy-nine I think. He was going to the local off-licence to get his Guinness which he and my mother used to have before they retired, and the off-licence was only about 100 yards down the road on the other side, so he had to cross the road. He got his Guinness to take home and he met a friend on his way back and had a chat to him. This would have been around about 8 o'clock in the evening and, having had the chat, he said cheerio and stepped off the kerb and a car came along. This would have been about 50 to 100 yards away from the house. It ran over him and killed him, and made such an impact that it was very difficult to recognise him. The ambulance came and took him away but he was dead at the time. I don't think he had anything in his pockets to substantiate who he was but at around 11 o'clock that evening they found out who he was.

Now over that period of three hours I just try and imagine what went through my mother's mind. There was Dad just going down to the off-licence which was only 100 yards away, which would only take him about ten minutes, and there it was 11 o'clock and he hadn't come back. She was getting very concerned at the time and I suppose she didn't know what was happening or what was going on until a policeman called at the house at 11 o'clock and told her the tragic news. My brother and sisters were advised and they came round to be with my mother. They immediately set about phoning me the bad news which I heard at around about 11 o'clock in the morning, which was allowing for the 12 hours delay. I was in the shop working at the time and I had to call my wife down to take over the shop. I went home for a few hours to get over the sudden shock which I had received.

My father was a great man. I always thought he was a good man and a good father. He was very strict. He liked his visits to the pub with his pals. He was a hard worker and I considered him to be a good provider. He was a very fit man and he was seventy-nine years of age when he was killed, and he was still working. I can always recollect going back to when he was at the age of sixty-five. He said, 'Well, Fred, I think I will do another five years work and stay on until I am seventy.' Now working at the gas works shift work there was a 6-2, 2-10 in the night work, alternately. I didn't think it was good enough for a person at that age to carry on doing extra time and I said to him, 'Look your health is very good; you're a very active man. You can actually retire from this job and take your pension and get yourself a part-time job daily work somewhere. There's plenty of people looking for active retired people with your ability.'

Well, thankfully, he listened to me and he packed up his job. He had several jobs, mainly working at petrol stations either doing the accounts or looking after the newcomers or pumping petrol for the customers that came in. As I say, he was a very, very active man. I remember him saying to me some months afterwards, 'You know, I have never been so well off in all my life. I am very happy and contented and I am very glad that I didn't carry on.'

I said, 'Well, if you had carried on and done another five years there you probably wouldn't have lasted that long.'

Anyway, it was sad because I wasn't able to see him although I had been over once. I had taken my family and we had all made our peace with one another and it was a tragedy to lose one of your parents. I know this happens to everybody as they get on in life but it is always sad when it happens. My mother never really recovered from it. She looked after herself for a while but I think the loneliness of losing a life companion gradually got the better of her and she had to go into hospital for one or two sicknesses. She eventually just died naturally at around the age of seventy-eight, about four years after my father died. These were two tragedies that happen to everybody I know, but they are always doubly bad when they happen to you.

So we carried on with life and, of course, I still had all my brothers and sisters alive at the time and progressively going through the different stages of my work. The paint shop, as I've said, was a problem. It was not providing the sort of income that I expected; and, as I said previously, the business was sold.

CHAPTER TEN

It was then that we decided to move to Taupo. Taupo was always a great attraction to us because of the trout fishing and as a holiday resort it was a very attractive place to go to. I thought at the time that this might be a good idea and so my wife and I agreed that we would do just that. I suppose that right throughout our life we had moved from place to place. We had always been happy doing it, as long as we were doing things together and we had a very nice family at the time. Our children were growing up and we then moved on our way at Taupo. We sold our house and bought another one on the hill in Taupo overlooking the lake. The house was quite a modern one, in the street called Henry Hill Road, with central heating and all the mod cons.

I set about getting myself a job which was no problem in Taupo because as it happened I walked into a retail outlet called the Auckland Glass Company, which was a retailer in wallpaper, paint and all subsidiary lines, and, immediately I walked in with the experience that I'd had, the boss wanted me to start straight away. I know that I started within a couple of days. One or two of my friends moved into Taupo at the same time, so we were able to carry on our close relationship with them as well. I enjoyed my work in the paint company but once again this was working for a boss. Not that I was against working for bosses but I always felt that I had a better ability than to work on what I call a weekly wage, and I was always on the lookout for something that I could do better at.

There came a period of time when my wife had to go to Auckland to visit some friends of ours, and she'd gone for a week with the children, it being the children's holidays. I carried on working and I happened to peruse the daily paper. I saw what was called a blind ad for a salesman for a company with good prospects of remuneration and commissions, and so on. I don't know but the ad seemed to attract me so I got in touch with these people by phone and by good fortune the chap who was doing the interviewing was in the Travel Lodge at Rotorua at the time, and my wife still being away, I was going up on Saturday to meet her, so he agreed to stay overnight. As I drove to Rotorua on my way to Auckland we would have breakfast at the Travel Lodge and discuss the prospects of the job. It happened to be with a building and banking society called the Southern Cross Building and Banking Society at the time, which was quite a big organisation, and we had our breakfast and discussed the prospects of the job. Apparently he liked the look of me and my experience, and I then went for a further interview in Auckland in Victoria Street. I had the interview with the sales manager and one of the problems was, they thought probably my age might be against me for the job. I had reached the age of fifty-five then, but with the experience that I had they decided that they would give me the opportunity as sales representative for the company which was virtually in the area that I lived, taking in Tokoroa, Turangi, Taupo, Reporoa and surrounding areas.

I set about studying the plan. I went to a sales-course meeting and very quickly got aligned to what the prospects of the job were, whether I understood it so that I could sell it to the public. It was virtually a savings plan with opportunities of interest-free and interest-bearing loans. Virtually all that people were doing was saving money but with the prospects of gaining finance. The company had a very good reputation and I enjoyed having the pleasure of working with them. I caught on to it very quickly apparently, and my sales figures proved that I had the ability to handle it so much so that in any competitions that were coming up at that time for different items, I was always amongst the prize winners, either the top salesman or within the first two or three.

It wasn't a pressure job at all; it was one that I enjoyed and it produced a marvellous income. I was picking up somewhere around about $350 to $400 a week when the average wage was way, way below that. My wife couldn't believe this; she said it would never last, the sort of income I was getting. I never worked on a Friday because I always considered it was a bad selling day. I dealt mostly with business people and farmers and most people on Friday were thinking about what they were going to do for the weekend rather than thinking about business. So I only worked four days to accrue all this income. It didn't take very long for the company to recognise my ability and promoted me to a supervisor of a new superannuation fund that they were starting, and this got off the ground and became fairly successful. In this time I decided, because of the job, that I would move to Auckland and we had only been in Taupo then about eighteen months. We moved to Auckland to be nearer the centre of the operations and the company agreed it would be better for me although they did not contribute anything towards the move. It was completely on my own initiative I decided to do this and we found a very nice house in Ridge Road in Browns Bay overlooking the Waitemata, a delightful spot and things got going well. The superannuation fund was doing well and I was away two or three days a week at different times. Bear in mind that my brother-in-law was still with us, and he was great company for my wife when I was away for these couple of days. The children settled down to their new schools and everything seemed to be very fine.

After about nine months I was called into head office with the assistant sales manager. Well they said, 'Fred, we are going to offer you an opportunity here but we will not be offended if you refuse it. We realise you have only just moved and this is going to necessitate you moving again.'

They offered me a position, as sales manager for the lower half of the North Island. The remuneration would be very, very good, which it was. They would pay all my legal expenses, pay all my moving and give me time off and fly me down to Wellington to look for another home. They said, 'There is no rush, just if you can give us an answer within a week, that would be fine.'

So anyway, I walked out with my head a bit dizzy at the time I suppose, being offered such a high position with the company. I went home to my wife and we sat down and had lunch. We talked about it and she said, 'Well, what do you want to do?'

'Well, the most important thing is what do we want to do together,' I said. 'The only comment I will make is, opportunities like this are once in a lifetime but I will only do it if it has the full cooperation of yourself and that you are quite happy to do it.'

She said, 'Well, whatever you do, I am happy to do.'

She was a woman like that; she knew that I didn't make silly moves and that everything I tried to do was constructive, and she was quite happy to do this. So I went back that afternoon and saw the sales manager and accepted the position, and we all shook hands on it. Then we had to set about selling our house. That evening I happened to meet the representative of the real estate on my way home and I called in to see him and I said, 'I have got a house for you to sell.'

He said, 'That's good. Where is it?'

I told him – number 8 Ridge Road.

He said, 'But I've only just sold it to you!'

I said, 'That's right, but it's on the market. I've just got a transfer and I've got to get away as soon as you can sell it.'

Well, he came along the next morning at 7.45 before I was due to leave for the office and he brought a young lawyer to look at the house. I think I had put about $2,000 on top of what the house had cost me. I had only been there nine months and before I'd left the sale was accepted and we had the house sold. The big shock was when I walked back into the office and I told them the house was sold, and they couldn't believe it. They said, 'My God, you're a quick worker aren't you?'

The next job was to proceed down to Wellington and see what the housing situation was like down there. I happened to be reading the *New Zealand Herald* and, fortunately enough, in the real estate section I saw a house for sale in Raumati which is around about twenty-seven, twenty-eight miles north of Wellington. It was my intention, anyway, not to go and live in the highly populated areas of Wellington and plus the fact that Wellington didn't have what one would call good weather. When the weather was bad, it was very, very bad. You only had to travel twenty-five or twenty-seven miles north of Wellington and you came into a very different set of climatic conditions altogether. The Kapiti coast, of course, is renowned for its sunshine and in most cases it had some of the highest sunshine rates in New Zealand.

However, my wife and I proceeded down to Wellington to meet this real estate agent who then promptly took us up to have a look at this house in Raumati. It was a newish-type home, a split-level on a very good section, fairly well elevated. A three-bedroom home, it had a beautiful lounge. It was empty at the time so we could evaluate it much better. The condition of the house was excellent. It didn't need any work done on it. It didn't have central heating which we proceeded to put in immediately we arrived there. So, anyway, after spending an hour looking round the house we looked at one another and we said, 'Well what more do we want?' We had to be perfectly honest, it had everything. We had two children, the schools were handy and the shopping area was close at hand. It was handy to the motorway which wasn't too far away for my getting backward and forward, and it had everything we wanted, so we said, 'Look, that's it; we'll take it.'

We duly signed the contract for the house and once again surprise, surprise, I told the company of my position and that the move could take place very quickly. We put everything into operation, transfer of mortgages, and got the removal people into operation and in the matter of inside a month we had moved and we were in Raumati. Now the job I had to do was quite a big job actually. The particular area covered from New Plymouth across to Napier, everything south of the North Island. It had been run-down because of the lack of supervision being quite some distance away from the head office. Its sales figures were very poor by comparison and not a very good staff clientele there. So it was my job to adjust all this, remove the dead wood, inject new people into the organisation with good training schedules, and so on. Vehicles were available to me to apportion to the agents who I thought were going to be successful. It would be true to say that within twelve months I finished up with a very good, efficient team – a team of around about twenty-five agents which included four or five supervisors and myself – so much so that we did eventually happen to become the top area on one occasion and had good placings on all the others. So it was a personal achievement for myself and the team that I had down there, and it turned out to be a reasonably happy time. There were several occasions I had one or two awkward individual cases to attend to as regard what I call undesirable members of the company, which we had to very subtly dispose of. This was done and, as I say, by the time I had finished there and completed my assignment we had a top area. The family settled down well. We built a large swimming pool in the front of the house. It is very difficult to describe this when you say put the swimming pool in the front. It was a sunken area, secluded away from the street and surrounded by trees and shrubs where we put the swimming pool, which was ideal. We could almost swim ten months of the year because it was very well protected from the elements of any bad weather that we had, and of course the family enjoyed this and, with invitations of friends to barbecues and things like that, we had a most enjoyable time.

After about three years, of course, further promotions came along and I was then made the recruiting and training officer for the whole company for the North and South Island and this did require a move up to Auckland again which everybody was quite happy to do. I think we had got quite used to moving around. We enjoyed it; it didn't become a problem to us. Every move became a challenge, a new environment for us and by this method we got to know New Zealand very well. On this occasion when our move came, which was to have been my last one with the company, I decided to move to Pukekohe which was round about thirty-five miles south of Auckland.

Once again, we steered clear of the main cities and got into the rural areas where we could enjoy life when we were away from the company. Pukekohe is an agricultural area with a population of around about 11,000 or 12,000 people. Well-renowned for its agricultural work, which it does in the form of kiwi fruit, fruit such as apples, oranges, persimmons, it also grows ordinary vegetables like the domestic vegetables and is very well-known for its potatoes.A very nice area, rolling country, it always reminded me of Devon in England. I think this was one of the reasons why we went there. We got a very nice home in Pukekohe, which we enjoyed. We were there for the time that I lasted with the company.

CHAPTER ELEVEN

We always tried to get away each year. One year we did a tour around the Islands looking at Samoa, Fiji, Tonga and Sydney which we thoroughly enjoyed. On this particular occasion we decided that we would go to America and plans were made in the latter part of 1980 to explore one of our first trips to America. It was around about the 20th December that we flew out from Auckland to Los Angeles, which was a great experience and also wonderful for the children. They enjoyed Disneyland and Knottsberry Farm and the museums and everything that Los Angeles had to offer. We had a wonderful time there. We stayed there for about eight or nine days before we decided to move on, and then we decided that we would take a tour as far round as California and beyond, where the weather was good. Remembering that on the Eastern seaboard of America it was very, very cold weather whilst all around California areas it was almost equivalent to our summer weather, and we were getting very good temperatures where we could still swim in the sea or outside swimming pools and run around in our bathing costumes, and have barbecues and jacuzzies.

We then decided it was time to move on and the idea was to see as much as we could of America in the short time that we had for our holiday. We travelled to San Diego where we went to one of the big wildlife zoos where the animals are bought up in their natural environment. We thought this was very good and enjoyed it immensely. Then we went down the borders and pursued our way along the border of America, and a couple of times we went into Mexico and enjoyed the experience there. One can understand why so many of the Mexicans try to get across the border because the standard of living was dramatically lower than in the

USA itself. However, it was quite a unique experience and we enjoyed it.

Christmas Day was spent in the Arizona desert at a place called Yuma. Once again quite an experience as I never thought there was so much desert running around. I thought all the deserts were in Africa but here we were surrounded by sand. There were warnings of sandstorms everywhere. We spent our Christmas Day, as I said, in Yuma and Christmas Evening was spent at a hotel. They put on special evenings there with entertainment. It is amazing how many American people go out for their Christmas Evenings. This was a delightful evening with the American food and the entertainment; quite a unique experience for everybody and we thoroughly enjoyed it.

We then proceeded on to Phoenix where we had distant relatives. We told them we were coming, and we spent a few days there enjoying ourselves and catching up with the magnificent modern city of Phoenix, the vast shopping complexes, its lifestyle and the beautiful homes they had there. Every home had a swimming pool and all the mod cons. It was quite an eye-opener as far as we were concerned to have a look at the different lifestyles of the people. We spent our New Year's Day there at a London club which was made up of people of English origin who had come from London. We saw the old year out and the new year in on this particular event and once again it was an enjoyable day.

We decided it was time to move on after a while. We said we would be coming back on our way back through. We wanted to get down as far as Tucson thinking that this was probably as far as we would go eastward because, as I mentioned before, the weather on the Eastern seaboard was very cold and there was a hell of a lot of snow about but we were still enjoying what we call relatively good summer weather. We arrived at Tucson and Tucson, I suppose I always think, is a dual city. There is the modern city of Tucson with its skyscrapers and a few miles down the road there is the old Indian-type city which is built purposely for the Western films that were made in those days. It was complete with the stations and shops and banks in the old Western style and we could see films being made there, or different sections of films being made while we were there, and we had a wonderful time. It was a terrific experience to live in a lifestyle of America 50 years ago.

On that morning we came back to Phoenix to meet our relatives for the last time and have lunch with them, and at that stage I decided to ring up the Highway Patrol to get some indication of what the weather was like at the Grand Canyon. Bearing in mind that we still had quite a journey to go and we did know there was a lot of snow up there. However, we had a long talk with the Highway Patrol and they asked where we came from, and we said, 'New Zealand.'

They said, 'Well, you just can't miss our Grand Canyon. As far as we're concerned there won't be any more snow until Monday and the roads are clear although there is plenty of snow up there. I am sure you will have a wonderful trip.'

So I put the phone down and said to the family, 'Right, the Grand Canyon it is.'

We duly said goodbye to our friends and set out on our way to the Grand Canyon. This was around about a four to five hour journey and after a time of travelling on level ground we decided to drive up the height of the Grand Canyon, bearing in mind that the Grand Canyon is 7,000 feet plus above sea level. We were making our way to a city called Flagstaff, which was very close to the Grand Canyon. We reached the area where the snow was lying in the fields and the roads were pretty packed with solid ice and driving along quite comfortably in our little pinto and enjoying the scenery. Suddenly, yours truly, had a terrific shooting of pain across his chest and ribs. I realised what had happened because I had seen it on television some time before. I had the presence of mind to be able to stop the car quickly and I got out and started walking away from it. My wife came up to me and said, 'What's wrong?'

I said, 'God, I feel terrible. I've got pains across my chest and my arms.' Stupidly I lit a cigarette but took only one puff and threw it down. Of course, my wife hadn't driven in America – let alone on the right side of the road and driving in this snowbound area. Being the woman that she was, she quickly adapted herself in the emergency and she drove the car for the next ten miles into Flagstaff. We booked into a motel and the owner said, 'Look, you had better get your husband into a hospital.'

They are aware of what happens when you get up there because in all the rooms there are little notices that say beware of heart attacks because of the rarefied air up there and as the surgeon said to me, 'That is what they are there for – to catch you people when you come up.'

Anyway, I went into the examination room and he said, 'We will fear the worst; we'll start at the top and see what we come across.'

Well, immediately they came across a cardiac arrest; I'd had a heart attack. They put me into an intensive care ward and plugged me up to all the cardiac machines and oxygen with plugs all over my body. I was a rare sight after a couple of hours. He called my wife in and we sat around the bed talking, and he said, 'Well, you have had a cardiac arrest and the only thing we found in your bloodstream was carbon monoxide poisoning.'

This was obviously caused by smoking and, of course, being in a closed-in car plus the fact that we were getting up into the rarefied air, really, I was a candidate for one of these attacks. However, the hospital treatment was tremendous and they gradually improved the situation so that after six days I was taken out of intensive care and put into an ordinary ward and after eleven days I was allowed to proceed out of the hospital.

In the meantime, we had a tremendous experience of meeting the American hospitality. The methodist minister came and saw me the next day and had a long chat with me and wanted to know about my family who were there. He immediately set about making arrangements for people to look after my wife and children and, although they had the horrendous experience of having me in hospital, almost close to death at one stage, they were looked after in the kindest way. People took my wife and children under their wing. They took them all over the Grand Canyon and took them to their homes and tenpin bowling. You name it, everybody had a very good time under such trying conditions.

I went through terrific remorse at the time knowing that it was cigarettes that had probably accentuated my particular problem. I suppose I had spent many times over the past years trying to curb smoking.

Pressure of work, tension and so on kept me smoking. As I say, I tried many different types of treatment but never had the willpower to give up smoking. Thinking back, in hospital, that I nearly killed my family through the stupidity of smoking it was one of the easiest jobs in the world for me to stop smoking. I never again had another cigarette and in a matter of weeks I detested the smell of it. It is a pity that it had to reach that stage for me to pack up smoking but I think it was probably provident that I had been in America and that I had been under circumstances which brought this about because I don't think it would have happened at ground level. I would still have been smoking and had reasons to complain about health in some other form related to smoking, so, as I say, I have never put a cigarette to my lips since and have no desire to, and try to encourage people not to smoke if it is at all possible. This was somewhere around fourteen years ago when this happened. People often say to me, 'How did you manage to pack up smoking so easily?'

I say, 'Well, when you have had the wits scared out of you in the manner that I did it is a very simple matter. That is the simplest answer that I can give.'

I went back to the church on the Sunday before I left to thank the minister and to thank the people who had helped my wife and children whilst I was in hospital. I felt very humble for the hospitality they had shown. They were only too pleased and were happy to see that I was on the road to recovery. One family insisted that they took us to the station when we were to depart the next day and I accepted it because we had given up our car at that time. I thought it was better that I didn't carry on driving.

We decided to go back to Los Angeles by train. They duly picked us up at our motel and took us down to the station at around 7 o'clock to get on the train at 7.30 p.m. I was immediately advised that the train had been delayed because of the snow conditions on the Eastern seaboard in America. It was coming through from New York and had been held up because of the snow and wouldn't arrive in Flagstaff until about 3.30 the next morning. Once again, the American hospitality came to the fore.

I said, 'Well, you go on your way; you have got to go to work the next day.'

They said, 'No, way; you come with us.'

So they took us home and lit a massive great log fire. It was a beautiful home. They bought some friends around to entertain us. We talked about New Zealand and they talked about America and the time went very quickly. The children were entertained by games and what have you, and at 3 o'clock they took us to the station where we finally departed. I couldn't thank them enough for what they did. Bearing in mind these people had to go to work that morning and they gave up all their time to see that we were entertained. I find it very hard to believe that I would get that hospitality anywhere else. I suppose you would but, however, they were very, very nice people. I was very pleased to get on that train and get back to sea level where there was plenty of oxygen. I was recovering very well. I took the doctor's advice to do plenty of exercise, walking et cetera, and I found myself recovering very quickly. We enjoyed our holiday at a little slower pace but, nevertheless, we did enjoy it and finally concluded it satisfactorily.

People at home knew what had happened because my wife had advised most people that we'd had this problem and she didn't know what the end was going to be. Fortunately, we arrived home in one piece and we set about going through a complete recuperation. I went back to my work to introduce myself back to them and they insisted that I didn't return until I was fully recovered. I went under the specialist while I was there to check my health and he went through giving me a series of examinations, and after a period of about three months he said, 'Well, Mr Holt, if I hadn't seen these records your body doesn't indicate to me at all that you have had a heart attack and you have completely recovered. Forget about everything and go on living your life normally and you shouldn't have any further problems.'

I never have and the treatment that I had in America and looking after myself, being thankful I suppose that I have always kept myself reasonably fit, I made a complete recovery and I had no recurrence, and I don't expect to. As I have said before, I don't smoke and I am thankful that I had the sense enough to give it up. It could be a certain amount of providence. No doubt about it, if I had carried on smoking the way I was doing it would have shown itself by some other sort of problems.

CHAPTER TWELVE

I carried on my work until I was about sixty-five and then I decided to retire from the pressure of work that we were having and duly resigned from my job. Not being prepared for retirement, this was the next minor problem I suppose. It became quite a problem to my wife and myself that, apart from my normal hobbies I had around the house, I was getting up in the morning with nowhere to go. Needless to say, it wasn't long before I went back to work again and I went to work for a real estate company in Pukehohe and did very well. Another new challenge which I succeeded in I suppose but after six months I realised I was back to square one, working seven days a week, so I immediately gave that up. I did come to terms gradually with retirement. I took up bowls which was another little challenge for me. I like my gardening, my hydroponics, etc., and we settled down to a reasonably good retirement life.

In that time we went back to England and had a wonderful time, just my wife and I. Our children at this stage were working or married, and we didn't have problems of taking children with us, and we had a great eight weeks' holiday, one of the highlights, I suppose, of our holidays away. Our relatives were extremely good to us and we spent very many happy times with them.

We came back home and a couple of years after that, this would be around about 1986, my wife was complaining of problems internally. We were not too sure what they were but various visits to the doctor's and various tests indicated that there was nothing wrong with her seriously, and there were occasions when she had to keep going back to the doctor, so much so that she felt very guilty about going. She said, 'They must think I am a bit of a malingerer.' We were always aware that her mother had died of cancer when she was about seventy and we were consoled by the fact that the doctors had indicated to us that there was nothing wrong with her. We felt happy about this and it got to the stage where she became terribly worried. I said that the best thing to do was to ask the doctor for a second opinion, which she did. She went to see a specialist in Papatoetoe and on examination he had her put into hospital. Within twenty-four hours, he was operating on her. This was a shock, but however, she went into Middlemore for this operation to have a hysterectomy and on the morning after the operation the doctor rang me and said the operation was a total success. There was a cancer growth which they had removed and as far as he was concerned my wife would make a total recovery and he said, 'I am pretty happy that this was a complete success.'

She was in hospital, I suppose, for possibly another fortnight and we were able to take her home. On one of the final visits to the doctor as a check-up he said, 'I would just like one thing. I would like you to have one of these computer X-rays. They dissect the body in its different parts.'

It was quite expensive at the time; it cost me $460 to have this examination and I was quite happy to get the peace of mind that everything was OK. We duly arrived at this particular establishment for the examination. As I said, it was a private examination by a private hospital and you were actually given the result straight away. She went through for the X-rays and came out. We sat there for about an hour and the doctor came out and said, 'Well, Mrs Holt, I wish I could tell everyone such good news as I have got for you. You have no problems at all. Everything is 100 per cent.'

We duly paid over our $460 and gave one another a big hug and walked away on cloud nine. It was at that time that I said to my wife about going for another holiday and where would we go. I said to her, 'What about England? Would you like to go back to England?'

All our relatives were there and we liked the English countryside, the English way of life although we had never had the desire to go back and live there permanently.

She said, 'Yes, I would.'

So I made the arrangements for us to go on another holiday as our winter approached, I think about the middle of July. Shortly after this she didn't feel things were a hundred per cent, so we ended up going to the Auckland Oncology Department which is the top department in cancer with all the top doctors. She underwent several tests at different times. And it was about this time I said to the surgeon, 'We have booked for a holiday. I don't care whether we go or not but I do have to make a decision this week as to whether we shall be going so I would like your advice.'

He said, 'Look, Mr Holt, there is no reason why you shouldn't take your wife on a holiday. It will do her the world of good and I'm sure everything will be fine.'

So I went back and confirmed the holiday, paid the rest of the money and what have you.

Within three or four days after examinations and things they located, they decided to take my wife into the operating theatre and have another look at her. On this particular occasion she was back in Middlemore hospital under the same surgeon that performed the original operation. At 9.30 I had the tragic news from the doctor telling me that he had examined my wife and felt that there was nothing that he could do for her as the cancer had spread right throughout her body. This was a shock because we had done everything. We had had the special X-rays, we had doctors' confirmation that she was all right and there was the situation that they knew nothing until they operated on her. The shock was almost too much for me to overcome. However, they told me that she had about another fortnight to live. She knew this when I went and saw her, although we never spoke of it. We knew that the inevitable was going to happen. I had to advise all my family, my son and daughter.

This is the occasion where the bottom drops out of your life and you just don't know where to turn. I went back to the Auckland hospital and said to them, 'If there is nothing more you can do for her then I think the best thing to do is to take her home and I will care for her myself.' This we did. We brought her home and they had a special bed brought down from the hospital for her and she was back under the medical doctor who set her up on morphine treatment – a special attachment which automatically fed into her the correct amount of morphine so that she didn't suffer any undue pain, and she lasted for about a fortnight. On June 20th of that year she passed away during the night. I would like to say she died peacefully, having gone into a coma beforehand. There is not much more you can say about such a tragic happening when you lose a partner you have loved for thirty-nine years but I had to accept the inevitable that I had to carry on without her.

My daughter eventually moved to Taupo where they took on a holiday cafeteria business. Her husband was a chef. On friends advice I decided to take the trip to England and, as I already had two tickets, I asked my son to join me. In hindsight it was not the best thing to do because, meeting all my relatives and all my wife's relatives when I arrived in England, I had to relive the whole experience over and over and over again. So, as I say, it was not a holiday in that respect that I could recover from the loss. I was reliving it all the time. Perhaps, it was a good thing that I was able to meet all the relatives while I was over there and explain to them.

Anyway, we had the holiday, came back, my son went back to work and I carried on a form of retirement on my own. I did have a few friends who I used to help out in Pukekohe and Waiuku. My son then said to me, 'Dad, what would you say if I wanted to go back to England to try my luck with one of the big saloon car racing companies?' He used to do a certain amount of work for the Warkinshaw racing team when they did their road racing in New Zealand and he would have liked to get established with one of the big racing teams as a prototype mechanic.

'Well,' I said, 'Son, look at it this way. If I was sick, would you go?'

He said, 'No.'

I said, 'Well, get on your bike and go while you're young.'

I didn't want to keep him back just to keep me company, so he duly went on his way to England and was able to get work with the Ford company as a prototype mechanic, building the rally cars for them and at the same time attending all their meetings in Corsica, Italy, San Remo,

South of France, Portugal and Spain. He has got a wonderful job and I am very pleased for him. He has now got a young lady, to whom he is engaged and he has bought a house near Chelmsford and built himself a very successful life which I am very proud of.

Myself, I carried on with my life, and for four years, I suppose, never took an interest in another woman, although I did move to Waiuku to a friend of my wife who had lost her husband at that time. I was going over there doing a lot of the gardening. She had a big house and she split it into two parts, and she said, 'Well, if you like you can have the other half of the house; that is, if you wish.'

I immediately left my own house and went over there, I think mainly for the company. I was living quite an isolated life and I carried on for about eighteen months living there, and as I say, not looking at any women or for the purpose of taking up another partner. It was about this time that I joined the Waipipi Bowling club. Previous to that I had played at Buckland near Pukekohe and Waiuku. I liked this small club and established myself with it and there happened to be a very nice lady there who I didn't know was a widow at that time. I just happened to be talking to her one day about myself and she indicated that she was also a widow. We got to know one another and became very close and found that we were compatible with one another. We enjoyed each other's company and it was a natural thing that it wasn't long before we decided that we would set up house and get married. She had four sons and four daughters-in-law and twelve grandchildren. I had to get myself associated with all the family, which I did, and this was two years ago when we decided to get married. This was one of the best things that ever happened to me because I am now living in complete harmony. We went to England for our honeymoon and I introduced her to all my family.

All I can say now, in conclusion, is that I am a very happy man. I have had some wonderful experiences and some traumatic experiences, and now, having reached the age of seventy-seven, I hope that I will proceed on to enjoy a good many years of life with the partner that I have got, Joyce. We are both extremely happy and I suppose there is not very much I can add.

Well, we have just about come to the end of the story from gaslight to satellite having spent just on eight decades of a very interesting fast-moving life. I was reading an amusing article just before I concluded this story which I think sums up the era in which I lived. It said that the senior citizen is someone who was around before the pill, the population explosion and that was before television, penicillin, antibiotics, microwave ovens, frozen foods, radar and credit cards, and time sharing meant togetherness, not a holiday apartment; men wearing earrings, and being stoned meant having rocks thrown at you. People got married before living together, hence the blushing bride – how very quaint can one be. To be gay meant to be merry and aids were for assisting, and I think that really sums up the period of gaslight to satellite. I've enjoyed going over the memoirs in this book and am surprised at how much I can remember. All I can hope is that everybody will get the same enjoyment reading it.